TEACHING

HARCOURT SCIENCE

RESOURCES

Harcourt School Publishers

Orlando • Boston • Dallas • Chicago • San Diego

www.harcourtschool.com

HARCOURT SCIENCE
Contents

School-Home Connections — TR1–31

Unit A, Chapter 1	How Plants Grow	TR1
Unit A, Chapter 2	Types of Animals	TR3
Unit B, Chapter 1	Where Living Things Are Found	TR5
Unit B, Chapter 2	Living Things Depend on One Another	TR7
Unit C, Chapter 1	Rocks, Minerals, and Fossils	TR9
Unit C, Chapter 2	Forces That Shape the Land	TR11
Unit C, Chapter 3	Soils	TR13
Unit C, Chapter 4	Earth's Resources	TR15
Unit D, Chapter 1	The Water Cycle	TR17
Unit D, Chapter 2	Observing Weather	TR19
Unit D, Chapter 3	Earth and It's Place in the Solar System	TR21
Unit E, Chapter 1	Properties of Matter	TR23
Unit E, Chapter 2	Changes in Matter	TR25
Unit F, Chapter 1	Heat	TR27
Unit F, Chapter 2	Light	TR29
Unit F, Chapter 3	Forces and Motion	TR31

Picture Cards — TR33–42

Writing in Science — TR43–44

Vocabulary Cards — TR45–68

Activities for Home and School — TR69–84

Maps, Charts, Patterns, Graphs

Physical Properties Chart	TR85
Flowchart	TR86
Venn Diagram	TR87
Computer Notes	TR88
K-W-L Chart	TR89
Web Organizer	TR90
Chart Organizer	TR91
Knowledge Chart	TR92
Prediction Chart	TR93
Project Planning Chart	TR94
1-cm Grid Paper	TR95
Triangular Prism	TR96
Rectangular Prism	TR97
Weather Map	TR98

Chapter Content

In science we are beginning a chapter that focuses on plants. Plants have specific needs that must be met in order for them to thrive and grow. These needs are covered in the chapter, along with a thorough exploration of the parts of plants, how plants make food, and the purpose and function of seeds.

Science Process Skills

Learning to **observe** carefully is one of the most important skills of science. Invite your child to take a walk in your neighborhood to look at plants. Ask your child to explain the process a seed goes through as it grows into a mature plant. Let your child point out and name the different parts of the plants you see. Record these observations in a notebook. Later in the year, take another walk, and record any differences you observe in the same plants.

Science Fun

Children's books about science can serve a double purpose. While entertaining young readers, they can also help clarify scientific concepts. This helps students reinforce what they are learning in the classroom.

From Seed to Plant by Gail Gibbons (Holiday House, 1993).

From Seed to Plant represents the transformation of seeds into full plants in clear and simple language. The book explores the intricate relationship between seeds and the plants that they produce. The colorful illustrations serve to expand the reader's understanding of the basic science of plants.

Activity Materials from Home

Dear Family Member:

In order to do the activities in this chapter, we will need some materials that you may have around your home. Please note the items to the right. If possible, please send these things to school with your child.

Your help and support are appreciated!

____ **brown paper bag**
____ **3 kinds of seeds**
____ **empty 0.5-L plastic bottle**
____ **twist ties**

Harcourt

La escuela y la casa

Harcourt Ciencias

Contenido del capítulo

Hoy comenzamos un capítulo de ciencias sobre las plantas. Las plantas tienen necesidades específicas que deben satisfacer para poder crecer y prosperar. Estas necesidades se presentan en el capítulo, a través de una exploración detallada de las partes de las plantas, cómo las plantas producen alimentos y el propósito y función de las semillas.

Destrezas del proceso científico

Aprender a **observar** detalladamente es una de las destrezas más importantes de las ciencias. Invite a su hijo(a) a caminar por su vecindario para observar las plantas. Pida a su hijo(a) que explique el proceso por el que pasa una semilla a medida que crece hasta que se convierte en una planta madura. Permita que su hijo(a) señale y nombre las diferentes partes de una planta que ve. Anote estas observaciones en un cuaderno. Más tarde durante el año, caminen por el vecindario nuevamente y anoten cualquier diferencia que puedan observar en las mismas plantas.

Diversión

Los libros infantiles sobre las ciencias pueden tener dos propósitos. Además de entretener a los lectores jóvenes, también pueden ayudar a clarificar conceptos científicos. Esto ayuda a los estudiantes a reforzar lo que aprenden en el salón de clases.

> *From Seed to Plant* de Gail Gibbons (Holiday House, 1993).
>
> *From Seed to Plant* de Gail Gibbons representa la transformación de las semillas en plantas en un lenguaje claro y sencillo. El libro explora la relación compleja entre las semillas y las plantas que producen. Las ilustraciones a color sirven para ampliar la comprensión de las ciencias básicas de las plantas.

Materiales de casa para la actividad

Querido familiar:

Para hacer las actividades en este capítulo, necesitaremos algunos materiales que tal vez tenga en la casa. Observe los artículos de la lista de la derecha. Si es posible, por favor envíe estas cosas con su hijo(a) a la escuela.

¡Gracias por su ayuda y su apoyo!

____ **bolsa de papel de color café**
____ **3 tipos de semillas**
____ **botella plástica vacía de 0.5L**
____ **alambritos**

School-Home Connection

Chapter Content

We are beginning a chapter on a number of important aspects of animals. Different kinds of animals have different needs, but all share the need for food, water, air, and shelter. Your child will learn to identify and distinguish between mammals, birds, amphibians, fish, and reptiles.

Science Process Skills

Most people make daily observations of the world around them. Real understanding, however, comes from thinking about observations and making **inferences** about what is observed. This game will help your child gather data and make a logical inference using that data, while reinforcing your child's understanding of the different types of animals.

Animal 20-Questions

Play a question game about animals with your child. Together, write some questions, such as Are you a mammal, a bird, or a reptile? Do you have fur or feathers? What kind of place do you live in? What do you eat? You can find more qualities of animals in your child's science book. One player chooses an animal to think of, the other asks the questions until the animal is identified.

ScienceFun

Children's books about animals can be entertaining as well as instructive. Accurate illustrations serve as an added learning feature. Children can add to the information they have gathered in the classroom by reading a book that complements a lesson.

Animal Senses: How Animals, See, Hear, Taste, Smell and Feel by Pamela Hickman (Kids Can Publishers, 1998).

Pamela Hickman has written a book on animal senses. *Animal Senses: How Animals, See, Hear, Taste, Smell and Feel* presents intriguing text and science activities. Readers will find plenty of information about how different animals not only see, hear, smell, taste, and feel what's around them, but also pick up on clues by sensing heat, electricity, and magnetic fields.

Read this book together with your child. Work together to make a list of all the ways animals gather information about the world around them.

Activity Materials from Home

Dear Family Member:

In order to do the activities in this chapter, we will need some materials that you may have around your home. Please note the items to the right. If possible, please send these things to school with your child.

Your help and support are appreciated!

____ **metal cans**
____ **cotton batting**
____ **rocks**
____ **gravel**
____ **dried fish food**

La escuela y la casa

Harcourt Ciencias

Contenido del capítulo

Hoy comenzamos un nuevo capítulo de ciencias sobre un número de aspectos importantes de los animales. Diferentes tipos de animales tienen diferentes necesidades, pero todos comparten las necesidades de alimento, agua, aire y refugio. Su hijo(a) aprenderá a identificar y a distinguir entre los mamíferos, las aves, los anfibios, los peces y los reptiles.

Destrezas del proceso científico

La mayoría de las personas hacen observaciones diariamente del mundo que los rodea. Sin embargo, la comprensión proviene del pensar sobre las observaciones y del hacer **inferencias** sobre lo que se observa. Este juego ayudará a su hijo(a) a recopilar datos, mientras refuerza la comprensión de su hijo(a) sobre los diferentes tipos de animales.

20 preguntas sobre animales

Juegue un juego de preguntas sobre los animales con su hijo(a). Escriban algunas preguntas como: ¿Eres un mamífero, un ave o un reptil? ¿Tienes pelaje o plumas? ¿En qué clase de lugar vives? ¿Qué comes? Usted puede encontrar más cualidades de los animales en el libro de ciencias de su hijo(a). Un jugador piensa en un animal y el otro jugador hace preguntas hasta que identifica el animal.

Diversión

Los libros infantiles sobre animales pueden ser tanto divertidos como instructivos. Las ilustraciones precisas sirven como una característica adicional de aprendizaje. Los niños pueden leer un libro que complemente una lección para agregar información que han recopilado en el salón de clases.

Animal Senses: How Animals, See, Hear, Taste, Smell and Feel de Pamela Hickman (Kids Can Publishers, 1998).

Pamela Hickman ha escrito un libro sobre los sentidos de los animales. *Animal Senses: How Animals, See, Hear, Taste, Smell and Feel* presenta un texto fascinante y actividades científicas. Los lectores encontrarán información completa no solamente sobre cómo animales diferentes ven, oyen, huelen, saborean y sienten lo que está a su alrededor sino también cómo recopilan pistas al percibir calor, electricidad y campos magnéticos.

Lea este libro con su hijo(a). Trabaje con su hijo(a) para hacer una lista de todas las formas en que los animales recopilan información sobre el mundo que los rodea.

Materiales de casa para la actividad

Querido familiar:

Para hacer las actividades en este capítulo, necesitaremos algunos materiales que tal vez tenga en la casa. Observe los artículos de la lista de la derecha. Si es posible, por favor envíe estas cosas con su hijo(a) a la escuela.

¡Gracias por su ayuda y su apoyo!

_____ **latas de metal**
_____ **algodón en rama**
_____ **rocas**
_____ **gravilla**
_____ **alimento seco para peces**

Chapter Content

Today we begin a new chapter in science. We will be learning about ecosystems—the places on Earth where living things are found. We will be studying different types of forest ecosystems, water ecosystems, and desert ecosystems. We will also be doing several activities, including observing environments to see what living and nonliving things can be found in each and making a model of a desert ecosystem.

Science Process Skills

Learning to **observe** carefully is an important skill in science. This activity will help your child develop his or her ability to observe.

Gather a number of different household objects, such as a comb, a brush, a book, a dish—things that you have around the house. Show them as a group to your child for about 15 seconds. Then cover the objects. See how many items your child can remember. Change the objects several times, and see if your child improves.

Science Fun

Whether you live in a rural, suburban, or urban area, you live in an environment that includes living and nonliving things.

What to Do

Pick out a small area and plan an observation walk. You might choose a nearby park, field, or forest, or you may just walk around your yard. Before you go on the walk, talk about the things you will be looking for, such as living things, nonliving things, and sources of food and water. Make a chart like this one that you can fill in as you walk.

Our Local Environment		
Living Things	Nonliving Things	Other Observations

As you take your walk, record your observations. Use your observations to write a short story describing something in your local environment.

Activity Materials from Home

Dear Family Member:

To do the activities in this chapter, we will need some materials that you may have at home. Please note the items at the right. If possible, please send these things to school with your child.

Your help and support are appreciated!

____ **wire clothes hanger**
____ **dried beans**
____ **plastic wrap**
____ **shoe box**
____ **small rocks**
____ **gravel**
____ **sand**

Harcourt

La escuela y la casa

Contenido del capítulo

Hoy comenzamos un nuevo capítulo de ciencias. Aprenderemos sobre los ecosistemas, los lugares de la Tierra donde se encuentran los seres vivos. Estudiaremos diferentes tipos de ecosistemas forestales, acuáticos y desérticos. También haremos varias actividades, que incluyen observar los medio ambientes para determinar qué seres vivos y no vivos se pueden hallar en cada uno y hacer un modelo de un ecosistema desértico.

Destrezas del proceso científico

Aprender a **observar** detalladamente es una destreza importante de las ciencias. Esta actividad ayudará a su hijo(a) a desarrollar su habilidad de observar.

Recopile diferentes objetos caseros como un peine, un cepillo, un libro, un plato, cosas que tiene en la casa. Muéstrelas a su hijo(a), en un grupo durante 15 segundos. Luego tape los objetos. Vea cuántos objetos puede recordar su hijo(a). Cambie los objetos varias veces y vea si su hijo(a) mejora.

Diversión

No importa si viven en una área rural, un suburbio o una área urbana, viven en un medio ambiente que incluye seres vivos y no vivos.

Lo que vas a hacer

Elige un área pequeña y planea una caminata de observación. Podrías elegir un parque, un campo o un bosque cercano o podrías caminar por tu patio. Antes de ir a caminar, habla sobre las cosas que buscarás como seres vivos, no vivos y fuentes de alimento y agua. Haz una tabla como ésta que puedas llenar mientras caminas.

Nuestro medio ambiente local		
Seres vivos	Seres no vivos	Otras observaciones

Mientras caminas, anota tus observaciones. Usa tus observaciones para escribir un cuento corto que describa algo en tu medio ambiente local.

Materiales de casa para la actividad

Querido familiar:

Para hacer las actividades en este capítulo, necesitaremos algunos materiales que tal vez tenga en la casa. Observe los artículos de la lista de la derecha. Si es posible, por favor envíe estas cosas con su hijo(a) a la escuela.

¡Gracias por su ayuda y su apoyo!

____ **gancho de alambre de ropa**
____ **frijoles secos**
____ **papel de plástico**
____ **caja de zapatos**
____ **rocas pequeñas**
____ **gravilla**
____ **arena**

School-Home Connection

Chapter Content

Today we begin a new chapter in science. We will be learning about the ways that living things depend on one another. Your child will learn how living things get food, and how all animals are in some way dependent on plants for food. This idea will be reinforced in activities in which students make model food chains and food webs, tracing the flow of energy from plants to animals.

Science Process Skills

Who Eats What?: Food Chains and Food Webs by Patricia Lauber and Holly Keller (Harpercrest, 1995).

Making accurate **observations** is an important science skill. Often, we directly observe the world around us. But sometimes, it is difficult to see all the steps in a process in nature. Use the book *Who Eats What?* to help your child make observations about how food energy moves from one living thing to another. After browsing through the book, have your child choose several food chains and trace with a finger the movement of energy from plants to animals to other animals.

Science Fun

A food chain is a model of how energy moves in the real world. You can use what your child observed in *Who Eats What?* to make personal food chains that include your family's favorite foods.

What You Need

- index cards
- yarn
- tape
- science book or other reference book

What to Do

1. Have your child draw pictures on index cards showing the chains for the things they eat, such as milk, which came from a cow, which ate grass. Connect the cards using yarn and tape.

2. Ask each family member to make a different food chain. After your child finishes Lesson 3, have him or her combine the chains to make a food web.

Activity Materials from Home

Dear Family Member:

To do the activities in this chapter, we will need some materials that you may have around your home. Please note the items listed at the right. If possible, please send these things to school with your child.

Your help and support are appreciated!

____ blank index cards
____ yarn or string
____ tape or glue
____ poster board

Harcourt

La escuela y la casa

Contenido del capítulo

Hoy comenzamos un nuevo capítulo de ciencias. Aprenderemos sobre las maneras en que los seres vivos dependen unos de otros. Su hijo(a) aprenderá cómo obtienen su alimento los seres vivos y cómo todos los animales dependen de una forma u otra de las plantas para alimentarse. Esta idea se reforzará en actividades en las que los estudiantes harán modelos de cadenas alimenticias y ciclos alimenticios, trazando el flujo de energía de las plantas a los animales.

Destrezas del proceso científico

Who Eats What?: Food Chains and Food Webs de Patricia Lauber and Holly Keller (Harpercrest, 1995).

Hacer **observaciones** precisas es una destreza importante de las ciencias. A menudo, observamos directamente el mundo que nos rodea. Pero a veces, es difícil ver todos los pasos en un proceso de la naturaleza. Use el libro *Who Eats What?* para ayudar a su hijo(a) a hacer observaciones sobre cómo se mueve la energía alimenticia de un ser vivo a otro. Después de hojear el libro, pida a su hijo(a) que elija varias cadenas alimenticias y trace con un dedo el movimiento de la energía desde las plantas hasta los animales y hasta otros animales.

Harcourt Ciencias

Diversión

Una cadena alimenticia es un modelo de cómo la energía se moviliza en el mundo real. Usted puede usar lo que su hijo(a) observó en *Who Eats What?* para hacer cadenas alimenticias propias que incluyan los alimentos favoritos de su familia.

Lo que necesitas

- tarjetas
- estambre
- cinta adhesiva
- libro de ciencias u otro libro de referencia

Lo que vas a hacer

1. Pida a su hijo(a) que haga ilustraciones en las tarjetas que muestren las cadenas para las cosas que comen como leche, la cual proviene de la vaca, que comió hierba. Una las tarjetas usando estambre y cinta adhesiva.

2. Pida a cada miembro de la familia que haga una cadena alimenticia diferente. Después de que su hijo(a) termine la Lección 3, pídale que combine las cadenas para hacer un ciclo alimenticio.

Materiales de casa para la actividad

Querido familiar:

Para hacer las actividades en este capítulo, necesitaremos algunos materiales que tal vez tenga en la casa. Observe los artículos de la lista de la derecha. Si es posible, por favor envíe estas cosas con su hijo(a) a la escuela.

¡Gracias por su ayuda y su apoyo!

_____ tarjetas en blanco
_____ estambre o hilo
_____ cinta adhesiva o pegamento
_____ cartón

Harcourt

School-Home Connection

Harcourt Science

Chapter Content

We are beginning a new chapter in science. We will be learning about the composition of the Earth, how rocks form, and fossils. We will explore the properties of minerals, classify rocks by the way they formed and determine one way the relative age of a fossil can be determined.

Science Process Skills

Comparing involves looking at two or more things and saying what is the same and what is different about them. In this chapter, students will compare igneous, sedimentary, and metamorphic rocks and discuss their differences and their similarities.

Encourage your child to start a collection of rocks gathered from your neighborhood or from areas to which you travel together. Help your child keep a rock collecting notebook, noting where and when different rocks are found. Have them compare the rocks in the collection and say how they are the same and different.

Science Fun

Children's books about rock collecting can be entertaining as well as instructive. Read the book together, then pick one or two of the activities below to try.

Let's Go Rock Collecting by Roma Gans and Holly Keller (Harpercrest, 1997).

- Pick one type of rock, and look for information about its formation, hardness, and uses.

- Have your child compare the cross-section of Earth to the information presented in his or her science book.

- Use your finger to trace the rise and eruption of lava in the cross-section of a volcano.

- Look for two children exploring a Roman road, finding fossils, mixing cement, and collecting rocks. Write a story about one of their adventures.

Activity Materials from Home

Dear Family Member:

In order to do the activities in this chapter, we will need some materials that you may have around your home. Please note the items to the right. If possible, please send these things to school with your child.

Your help and support are appreciated!

____ **modeling clay of different colors**
____ **seashells**
____ **wax paper**

Harcourt

La escuela y la casa

Harcourt Ciencias

Contenido del capítulo

Hoy comenzamos un nuevo capítulo de ciencias. Aprenderemos sobre la composición de la Tierra, cómo se forman las rocas y los fósiles. Exploraremos las propiedades de los minerales, clasificaremos rocas de acuerdo a la manera en que se formaron y hallaremos una manera de determinar la edad relativa de un fósil.

Destrezas del proceso científico

Comparar implica observar dos o más cosas y decir que en qué se parecen y en qué se diferencian. En este capítulo, los estudiantes compararán rocas ígneas, sedimentarias y metamórficas y comentarán sus diferencias y semejanzas.

Anime a su hijo(a) a que comience una colección de rocas que recoge en su vecindario o en áreas a las que hayan visitado. Ayude a su hijo(a) a que tenga un cuaderno de colección de rocas para que anote cuándo y dónde se hallaron las rocas. Pídale que compare las rocas de la colección y diga en qué se parecen y en qué se diferencian.

Diversión

Los libros infantiles sobre las colecciones de rocas pueden ser tanto divertidos como instructivos. Lean el libro y luego elijan una o dos de las actividades de abajo para probar.

Let's Go Rock Collecting de Roma Gans y Holly Keller (Harpercrest, 1997).

- Elige un tipo de roca y busca información sobre su formación, dureza y usos.

- Pida a su hijo(a) que compare el corte transversal de la Tierra con la información que se presenta en su libro de ciencias.

- Usa tu dedo para trazar el ascenso y la erupción de la lava en el corte transversal de un volcán.

- Busca dos niños que exploran un camino romano, buscan fósiles, mezclan cemento y recogen rocas. Escribe un cuento sobre una de sus aventuras.

Materiales de casa para la actividad

Querido familiar:

Para hacer las actividades en este capítulo, necesitaremos algunos materiales que tal vez tenga en la casa. Observe los artículos de la lista de la derecha. Si es posible, por favor envíe estas cosas con su hijo(a) a la escuela.

¡Gracias por su ayuda y su apoyo!

____ **plastilina de diferentes colores**
____ **conchas de mar**
____ **papel encerado**

Harcourt

School-Home Connection

Chapter Content

Our science class is beginning a chapter on Earth's landforms. Landforms are the shapes or features found on Earth's surface. They include mountains, valleys, canyons, plains, plateaus, and barrier islands. Weathering and erosion change landforms slowly. Volcanoes and earthquakes change landforms rapidly.

Science Process Skills

Drawing conclusions is an important science skill. To draw a conclusion, a scientist makes observations, collects data, and makes inferences about what the data mean. The scientist also thinks about what he or she already knows. When all of this information is considered, a conclusion about how something happened is drawn.

You can help your child practice drawing conclusions. Use several colors of clay or dough. Put the clay in layers, and then bend or fold the layers to make different shapes. Have your child observe the shapes, and then tell you what you did to make the shape. Have your child list the clues that led him or her to draw the conclusion about how the shape was made.

ScienceFun

Children's books about landforms can be entertaining as well as instructive. The following book will reinforce what your child is learning in the chapter, as well as provide a fun reading experience.

How Mountains Are Made by Kathleen Weidner Zoehfield and James Graham Hale (HarperTrophy, 1995).

In this book four children and a dog climb a mountain trail. Along the way, the characters explain Earth's structure. They discuss the different types of mountains and how they were formed.

After reading this book together, ask your child to choose one type of mountain and make a drawing detailing its formation. If you have clay available from the **Science Process Skills** activity, have your child make a model of the type of mountain he or she chose to draw.

Activity Materials from Home

Dear Family Member:

In order to do the activities in this chapter, we will need some materials that you may have around the house. Please note the items to the right. If possible, please send these things to school with your child.

Your help and support are appreciated!

____ sand
____ glass jar with lid
____ wax paper
____ baking soda
____ red, green, and blue food coloring
____ white vinegar

La escuela y la casa

Harcourt Ciencias

Contenido del capítulo

Hoy comenzamos un nuevo capítulo de ciencias sobre los accidentes geográficos. Los accidentes geográficos son las formas o características que se hallan en la superficie de la Tierra. Incluyen las montañas, los valles, los cañones, las llanuras, las mesetas y las islas de coral. La degradación y la erosión cambian los accidentes geográficos lentamente. Los volcanes y los terremotos cambian los accidentes geográficos rápidamente.

Destrezas del proceso científico

Sacar conclusiones es una destreza importante de las ciencias. Para sacar una conclusión, un científico hace observaciones, recopila datos y hace inferencias sobre lo que significa cada dato. El científico también piensa sobre lo que ya sabe. Cuando se considera toda esta información, se saca una conclusión sobre algo que ha sucedido.

Usted puede ayudar a su hijo(a) a que practique a sacar conclusiones. Use varios colores de plastilina o masa. Ponga la plastilina en capas y luego doble las capas para hacer diferentes figuras. Pida a su hijo(a) que observe las figuras y que luego le diga qué hizo usted para hacer esa figura. Pida a su hijo(a) que haga una lista de pistas que le permita sacar conclusiones sobre cómo se hizo la figura.

Diversión

Los libros infantiles sobre los accidentes geográficos pueden ser tanto divertidos como instructivos. El siguiente libro reforzará lo que su hijo(a) aprende en el capítulo, así como también proporciona una experiencia de lectura divertida.

How Mountains Are Made de Kathleen Weidner Zoehfield y James Graham Hale (Harper Trophy, 1995).

En este libro, cuatro niños y un perro escalan el sendero de una montaña. A lo largo del camino, los personajes explican la estructura de la Tierra. Comentan los diferentes tipos de montañas y cómo se formaron.

Después de leer este libro con su hijo(a), pídale que elija un tipo de montaña y que haga un dibujo detallado de su formación. Si tiene plastilina disponible de la actividad de **Destrezas del proceso científico,** pida a su hijo(a) que haga un modelo del tipo de montaña que ha elegido dibujar.

Materiales de casa para la actividad

Querido familiar:

Para hacer las actividades en este capítulo, necesitaremos algunos materiales que tal vez tenga en la casa. Observe los artículos de la lista de la derecha. Si es posible, por favor envíe estas cosas con su hijo(a) a la escuela.

¡Gracias por su ayuda y su apoyo!

____ **arena**
____ **frasco de vidrio con tapa**
____ **papel encerado**
____ **bicarbonato**
____ **colorante rojo, verde y azul**
____ **vinagre blanco**

Harcourt

School-Home Connection

Harcourt Science

Chapter Content

Our science class is beginning a chapter on soils. We will be learning that it takes a long time for new soil to form and why it is so important to conserve soil. We will be doing activities that focus on the parts that make up soil, the different types of soil, and ways plants help keep soil from washing away.

Science Process Skills

Predicting involves analyzing what you know and, based on that information, saying what you think will happen in the future. This activity can give your child practice in predicting outcomes.

Have your child predict whether each event listed below will help or hurt the soil. Have your child tell you why he or she made each prediction.

- A worm burrows in the soil. It leaves its wastes in the soil.

- A heavy rain washes soil from a farmer's field.

- A plant breaks a rock into small pieces.

- A gardener plants grass in a muddy area in her yard.

Science Fun

In Lesson 3, your child will be learning about different ways of slowing soil erosion. In this activity, you can build some model fields and test some soil conservation methods.

What You Need
- large rectangular baking pan
- watering can
- potting soil
- grass seed or sod

What to Do

1. Make a landscape out of soil in the pan. Include several hills and valleys.

2. Cover some of the hills with sod (or sprout grass seed on some of the hills). Leave some others bare.

3. Sprinkle water over your landscape, and observe how the grass affects the erosion of soil.

4. Expand your experiment. Make some terraces on your hills, or use different types of soil or different plants. Keep a record of how each change affected the rate of soil erosion.

Activity Materials from Home

Dear Family Member:

In order to do the activities in this chapter, we will need some materials that you may have around the house. Please note the items to the right. If possible, please send these things to school with your child.

Your help and support are appreciated!

____ **dry, unsweetened cereal**
____ **plastic wrap**
____ **paper plates**
____ **baking pans**
____ **large foam cups**

La escuela y la casa

Contenido del capítulo

Hoy comenzamos un nuevo capítulo de ciencias sobre los suelos. Aprenderemos que toma mucho tiempo para que se forme un suelo nuevo y por qué es tan importante conservar el suelo. Haremos actividades que enfocan las partes que forman el suelo, los diferentes tipos de suelo y las formas en que las plantas ayudan a proteger el suelo de ser arrasado.

Destrezas del proceso científico

Predecir implica analizar lo que sabes y basado en esa información, decir lo que crees que pasará en el futuro. Esta actividad le puede dar a su hijo(a) la práctica de predecir los resultados.

Pida a su hijo(a) que prediga si cada suceso en la lista de abajo ayudará o dañará el suelo. Pida a su hijo(a) que le diga por qué hizo esa predicción.

• La madriguera de un gusano en el suelo. Éste deja sus desperdicios en el suelo.

• Una lluvia fuerte arrastra el suelo de los campos de un agricultor.

• Una planta rompe una roca en pequeños fragmentos.

• Un jardinero siembra grama en un área fangosa de su jardín.

Diversión

En la Lección 3, su hijo(a) aprenderá sobre las diferentes formas de disminuir la erosión del suelo. En esta actividad, puedes hacer algunos modelos de campos y probar algunos métodos de conservación del suelo.

Lo que necesitas

• bandeja grande rectangular
• regadera de plantas y flores
• semillas de grama o césped
• tierra para plantar

Lo que vas a hacer

1. Elabora un paisaje hecho de la tierra en la bandeja. Incluye muchas colinas y valles.

2. Con su hijo(a), cubra algunas colinas con césped (o coloque semillas de grama en algunas colinas). Deje algunas descubiertas.

3. Rieguen con agua el paisaje y observen cómo la grama afecta la erosión del suelo.

4. Extiendan su experimento. Coloquen algunas terrazas en sus colinas o usen diferentes tipos de tierra o diferentes plantas. Anoten cómo cada cambio afectó el porcentaje de la erosión del suelo.

Materiales de casa para la actividad

Querido familiar:

Para hacer las actividades de este capítulo, necesitaremos algunos materiales que tal vez tenga en la casa. Observe los artículos de la lista de la derecha. Si es posible, por favor envíe estas cosas con su hijo(a) a la escuela.

¡Gracias por su ayuda y su apoyo!

_____ cereal seco y sin dulce
_____ papel de plástico
_____ platos de papel
_____ bandejas
_____ vasitos grandes de estireno

Chapter Content

Our science class is beginning a chapter on Earth's resources and ways to conserve those resources. We will learn that Earth holds many resources, some of which are renewable, and some of which are not. There are a number of ways to retrieve resources, including mining for gold and pumping oil.

Science Process Skills

Using numbers helps a person tell others exactly what data has been collected. You can give your child practice in using numbers by doing a pantry survey. Look through your kitchen cupboards and count the items made of aluminum (juice and soft-drink cans), steel (most canned items), and plastic. Work together to make a bar graph showing how many items of each kind you found. Discuss the resources needed to make these materials. Are any of them renewable? (Containers made from paper are made of renewable resources.)

ScienceFun

Children's books about conserving resources can be entertaining as well as instructive. You can find this book, or a similar book, at your local library.

Earth-Friendly Outdoor Fun: How to Make Fabulous Games, Gardens, and Other Projects from Reusable Objects by George Pfiffner (John Wiley & Sons, 1996).

Together with your child, browse through the 25 fun-to-do projects this book contains. The book includes step-by-step instructions on how to convert materials such as scrap cardboard and plastic bottles into items for outdoor fun and use. Projects include making games such as bowling and pick-up sticks, carrying out gardening activities, making a kite, making a giant bubble maker, and making a boomerang. Pick one of the projects to do.

Activity Materials from Home

Dear Family Member:

In order to do the activities in this chapter, we will need some materials that you may have around the house. Please note the items to the right. If possible, please send these things to school with your child.

Your help and support are appreciated!

____ **oatmeal-raisin cookies**
____ **paper plates**
____ **used, washed aluminum cans**
____ **large plastic trash bags**

Harcourt

La escuela y la casa

Contenido del capítulo

Hoy comenzamos un nuevo capítulo de ciencias sobre los recursos de la Tierra y la forma de conservar estos recursos. Aprenderemos que la Tierra tiene muchos recursos, algunos de los cuales son renovables y algunos de ellos no. Hay un número de maneras de salvar los recursos, incluidos la minería de oro y la extracción de petróleo.

Destrezas del proceso científico

Usar los números ayuda a las personas a decirle a otras exactamente los datos que se han recopilado. Usted puede hacer que su hijo(a) practique el uso de números al realizar una encuesta sobre la despensa. Busque en los armarios de su cocina y cuente los artículos hechos de aluminio (latas de jugos y de refrescos), de acero (la mayoría de los artículos enlatados) y de plástico. Trabaje con su hijo(a) para hacer una gráfica de barras y mostrar cuántos artículos de cada tipo encontró. Comente los recursos necesarios para hacer estos materiales. ¿Son renovables algunos de ellos? (Los recipientes hechos de papel son hechos de recursos renovables.)

Diversión

Los libros infantiles sobre la conservación de los recursos pueden ser tanto divertidos como instructivos. Usted puede encontrar este libro o un libro similar en su biblioteca local.

Earth-Friendly Outdoor Fun: How to Make Fabulous Games, Gardens, and Other Projects from Reusable Objects de George Pfiffner (John Wiley & Sons, 1996).

Junto con su hijo(a), hojee los 25 proyectos de cosas divertidas que contiene este libro. El libro incluye instrucciones paso por paso sobre cómo convertir materiales, como un pedazo de cartulina y botellas de plástico, en artículos de uso y diversión al aire libre. Los proyectos incluyen hacer juegos como el boliche y recoger palitos, llevar a cabo actividades de jardinería, hacer una cometa, hacer un soplador de burbujas gigante y hacer un bumerang. Elija uno de los proyectos y háganlo.

Materiales de casa para la actividad

Querido familiar:

Para hacer las actividades de este capítulo, necesitaremos algunos materiales que tal vez tenga en la casa. Observe los artículos de la lista de la derecha. Si es posible, por favor envíe estas cosas con su hijo(a) a la escuela.

¡Gracias por su ayuda y su apoyo!

_____ galletas de avena y pasas
_____ platos de papel
_____ latas de aluminio usadas y lavadas
_____ bolsas de plástico de basura grandes

Harcourt

School-Home Connection

Harcourt Science

Chapter Content

Today in science we begin a chapter about water. In this chapter your child will learn how much water covers Earth's surface, where most of Earth's water is found, and what the water cycle is.

Science Process Skills

Using numbers can help people accurately communicate the data they have collected. This activity will give your child practice in using numbers.

Find out how much water is lost by a dripping faucet. Set a faucet to drip. Place a large measuring cup underneath the faucet. Check the amount of water collected in 1, 5, and 10 minutes.

Repeat the activity, changing how fast the faucet drips. Help your child compare the data you collected by asking questions such as these.

- When did we collect the most water? (when the faucet dripped fastest)

- When did we collect the least water? (when the faucet dripped slowest)

- Why should water leaks and drips be stopped?

Science Fun

The movement of water from Earth's surface to the air and back is called the water cycle. Plants play an important part in this cycle. Plants absorb water from the ground and release it to the air through their leaves.

What You Need

- houseplant
- small plastic bag
- twist-tie or tape
- water

What to Do

1. Put a plastic bag around one leafy branch of the plant.

2. Tightly secure the bag with a twist-tie or tape.

3. Write down what the plant and bag look like. Draw pictures if you wish.

4. Water the plant, then place it in a well-lit spot.

5. After an hour again observe the plant. Compare what the bag looked like before and after this investigation. Have your child identify what is now on the inside of the bag (water).

Activity Materials from Home

Dear Family Member:

To do the activities in this chapter, we will need some materials that you may have at home. Please note the items at the right. If possible, please send these things to school with your child.

Your help and support are appreciated!

_____ masking tape
_____ four identical jars
_____ salt
_____ 2 jar lids

Harcourt

La escuela y la casa

Contenido del capítulo

Hoy comenzamos un nuevo capítulo de ciencias sobre el agua. En este capítulo su hijo(a) aprenderá cuánta agua cubre la superficie de la Tierra, dónde se halla la mayor cantidad de agua y cuál es el ciclo del agua.

Destrezas del proceso científico

Usar números puede ayudar a las personas a comunicar con precisión los datos que han recopilado. Esta actividad le dará a su hijo(a) la práctica de usar números.

Determine qué cantidad de agua se pierde al gotear un grifo. Abra un grifo para que gotee. Coloque una taza de medir debajo del grifo. Revise la cantidad de agua recopilada en 1, 5 y 10 minutos.

Repita la actividad cambiando la velocidad de las gotas del grifo. Ayude a su hijo(a) a comparar los datos que usted recopiló haciendo preguntas como éstas:

- ¿Cuándo recolectamos mayor cantidad de agua? (cuando el grifo goteó más rápido)

- ¿Cuándo recolectamos menor cantidad de agua? (cuando el grifo goteó más lento)

- ¿Por qué se deben detener las goteras y los escapes?

Diversión

El movimiento del agua desde la superficie de la Tierra hasta el aire y viceversa, se conoce como el ciclo del agua. Las plantas juegan un papel importante en este ciclo. Las plantas absorben el agua de la tierra y la liberan al aire a través de sus hojas.

Lo que necesitas

- plantas caseras
- alambrito o cinta adhesiva
- bolsa de plástico pequeña
- agua

Lo que vas a hacer

1. Coloque con su hijo(a) la bolsa de plástico alrededor de una rama frondosa de la planta.

2. Aseguren la bolsa atándola con un alambrito o cinta adhesiva.

3. Escriba con su hijo(a) cómo se ve la planta y la bolsa. Pueden dibujar si lo desean.

4. Rieguen la planta, luego colóquenla en un lugar con bastante luz.

5. Después de una hora observen la planta nuevamente. Comparen cómo se ve la bolsa antes y después de esta investigación. Pídale a su hijo(a) que identifique lo que hay ahora dentro de la bolsa (agua).

Materiales de casa para la actividad

Querido familiar:

Para hacer las actividades en este capítulo, necesitaremos algunos materiales que tal vez tenga en la casa. Observe los artículos de la lista de la derecha. Si es posible, por favor envíe estas cosas con su hijo(a) a la escuela.

¡Gracias por su ayuda y su apoyo!

_____ cinta adhesiva de papel
_____ cuatro frascos idénticos
_____ sal
_____ 2 tapas de frasco

Harcourt

School-Home Connection

Chapter Content

Our science class is beginning a chapter on observing weather. We will investigate the layers of the atmosphere, and discover that weather happens mostly in the atmosphere's lowest layer. We will be making our own thermometer to help us measure the temperature of the air. We will also investigate how weather measurements are combined on a weather map.

Science Process Skills

When scientists **compare,** they determine how two things are the same and different. You can use the daily newspaper to help your child compare weather conditions in different areas of the country.

Each day for a week, examine the weather page in your local paper. Note what the weather will be in your area and in your state. Pick a state or city to the west of you, and each day compare your weather to the weather in that location. Keep track of the weather in both locations. At the end of the week, see if you can find any trends. (Weather often moves from west to east in the United States.)

Science Fun

The weight of air presses down on everything on Earth's surface. This activity demonstrates an everyday use of air pressure.

What You Need
- clear plastic straw
- clean plastic jar with lid
- awl
- clay
- water

What to Do

1. Fill the jar with water. Use the straw to suck some of the water out of the jar.

2. CAUTION: Have an adult use an awl to poke a hole through the jar's lid. The hole should be just big enough for the straw to fit through.

3. Put the straw through the hole. Seal any gaps around the straw with clay.

4. Try to suck water up the straw.

Explanation: Air pressure forces water up a straw. When the jar is sealed, air can't press on the water. The straw doesn't work.

Activity Materials from Home

Dear Family Member:

To do the activities in this chapter, we will need some materials that you may have around your home. Please note the items listed at the right. If possible, please send these things to school with your child.

Your help and support are appreciated!

____ **paper towels**
____ **plastic cups**
____ **index cards**
____ **clear drinking straws**
____ **clay**

Harcourt

La escuela y la casa

Harcourt Ciencias

Contenido del capítulo

Hoy comenzamos un nuevo capítulo de ciencias sobre el clima. Investigaremos las capas de la atmósfera y descubriremos que el clima ocurre principalmente en la capa más baja de la atmósfera. Haremos nuestro propio termómetro para medir la temperatura del aire. También investigaremos cómo se combinan las medidas del tiempo en un mapa meteorológico.

Destrezas del proceso científico

Cuando los científicos **comparan** determinan en qué se parecen y en qué se diferencian dos cosas. Usted puede usar un periódico diario para ayudar a su hijo(a) a comparar las condiciones del tiempo en diferentes áreas del país.

Cada día durante una semana examine la página del tiempo en su periódico local. Observe cómo será el clima en su área y en su estado. Elija un estado o una ciudad que le quede al oeste y compare cada día su clima con el clima de esa localidad. Manténgase informado sobre el clima en las dos localidades. Al final de la semana, vea si puede hallar alguna tendencia. (El clima normalmente se desplaza del oeste al este en Estados Unidos.)

Diversión

El peso del aire presiona todo hacia abajo en la superficie de la Tierra. Esta actividad demuestra uno de los usos diarios de la presión del aire.

Lo que necesitas

- pajita de plástico transparente   • punzón
- frasco de plástico con tapa limpio
- plastilina

Lo que vas a hacer

1. Llena el frasco con agua. Usa la pajita para chupar un poco de agua fuera del frasco.
2. **CUIDADO:** Pide a un adulto que use un punzón para abrir un hueco a través de la tapa del frasco. El hueco debe ser justo del tamaño de la pajita para que ésta pase.
3. Coloca la pajita a través del hueco. Sella cualquier vacío alrededor de la pajita con plastilina.
4. Trata de chupar agua por la pajita.

Explicación: La presión del aire hace que el agua suba por la pajita. Cuando se sella el frasco, el aire no puede presionar el agua. La pajita no funciona.

Materiales de casa para la actividad

Querido familiar:

Para hacer las actividades en este capítulo, necesitaremos algunos materiales que tal vez tenga en la casa. Observe los artículos de la lista de la derecha. Si es posible, por favor envíe estas cosas con su hijo(a) a la escuela.

¡Gracias por su ayuda y su apoyo!

____ toallas de papel
____ vasitos de papel
____ tarjetas
____ pajitas de beber transparentes
____ plastilina

Harcourt

School-Home Connection

Harcourt Science

Chapter Content

In science we are beginning a chapter on Earth and its place in the solar system. We will be studying the nine planets in the solar system, how Earth's tilt causes seasons, and how the sun, moon, and Earth interact to cause the moon's phases and eclipses. The chapter ends with a discussion of stars and constellations.

Science Process Skills

For centuries, people have observed the stars. Through careful **observations,** scientists determined that the sun is at the center of our solar system, and that the planets revolve around the sun. In this activity, you can make your own observations of the stars.

One dark night, preferably when the moon is in new phase, go outside with your child and observe the stars. Try to get away from city lights or other light sources. Take paper and crayons and record some of the patterns of the stars you see in the sky. Try to count the number of stars in one small section of the sky. Find some traditional constellations, or make up some of your own. Have your child tell you what he or she knows about the stars.

Science Fun

Moonlight is not generated by the moon. Instead, moonlight is reflected sunlight.

What You Need
- flashlight
- dark T-shirt
- small hand mirror

What to Do

1. Put on the shirt. Darken the room.

2. Have your partner shine the light on the front of your shirt. Turn to the left.

3. When you are facing away from the flashlight, hold the mirror to the side of your body. Tilt the mirror until light shines on the dark side of your shirt.

4. Continue turning to the left. Watch how the light changes.

Explanation: In this activity, the light is the sun, the mirror is the moon, and the person in the tee-shirt is Earth. As Earth turns, a spot on the surface moves from day into night. Reflected light from the moon can illuminate the dark side of Earth, but not as much as the sun.

Activity Materials from Home

Dear Family Member:

To do the activities in this chapter, we will need some materials that you may have at home. Please note the items at the right. If possible, please send these things to school with your child.

Your help and support are appreciated!

____ **white paper**
____ **transparent tape**

Harcourt

La escuela y la casa

Harcourt Ciencias

Contenido del capítulo

Hoy comenzamos un nuevo capítulo de ciencias sobre la Tierra y su lugar en el sistema solar. Estudiaremos los nueve planetas del sistema solar, cómo la inclinación de la Tierra causa las estaciones del año y cómo el Sol, la Luna y la Tierra se afectan entre sí para producir las fases lunares y los eclipses. El capítulo finaliza con un debate sobre las estrellas y las constelaciones.

Destrezas del proceso científico

Durante siglos las personas han observado las estrellas. A través de **observaciones** detalladas, los científicos determinaron que el Sol se encuentra en el centro de nuestro sistema solar y que los planetas giran alrededor del Sol. En esta actividad usted puede hacer su propia observación de las estrellas.

En una noche oscura, preferiblemente cuando la Luna esté en su fase nueva, salga con su hijo(a) y observe las estrellas. Trate de alejarse de las luces de la ciudad u otra fuente de luz. Tome un papel y creyones y anote algunos de los patrones de las estrellas que ve en el cielo. Trate de contar el número de estrellas en una sección pequeña del cielo. Halle algunas constelaciones tradicionales o invente alguna. Pida a su hijo(a) que le diga qué sabe sobre las estrellas.

Diversión

La luz de la Luna no la genera la Luna. En cambio, la luz de la Luna es reflejada por la luz solar.

Lo que necesitas

- linterna
- un espejo pequeño de mano
- una camiseta oscura

Lo que vas a hacer

1. Ponte la camiseta. Oscurece el cuarto.

2. Pide a alguien que alumbre el frente de tu camiseta. Gira a la izquierda.

3. Cuando no estés de cara a la linterna, sostén el espejo al lado de tu cuerpo. Inclina el espejo hasta que la luz se refleje en el lado oscuro de tu camiseta.

4. Continúa girando hacia la izquierda. Observa como cambia la luz.

Explicación: En esta actividad la luz es el Sol, el espejo es la Luna y la persona con la camiseta es la Tierra. Mientras la Tierra gira, una parte de la superficie se mueve del día a la noche. La luz reflejada por la Luna puede iluminar el lado oscuro de la Tierra, pero no tanto como el Sol.

Materiales de casa para la actividad

Querido familiar:

Para hacer las actividades de este capítulo, necesitaremos algunos materiales que tal vez tenga alrededor de la casa. Observe los artículos de la lista de la derecha. Si es posible, por favor envíe estas cosas con su hijo(a) a la escuela.

¡Gracias por su ayuda y apoyo!

_____ papel blanco
_____ cinta adhesiva transparente

School-Home Connection

Harcourt Science

Chapter Content

Today in science we begin a chapter on the physical properties of matter. We will be examining physical properties—those things that can be observed with the senses. We will see how adding or taking away heat causes it to change state, and we will explore different ways to measure matter.

Science Process Skills

One way we learn about the materials around us is to **measure** them. This activity will give your child practice in making simple measurements of length and volume.

Gather a ruler, measuring cups of different volumes, and several rectangular boxes, such as a CD or audio tape cases and shoe boxes.

- Have your child use the ruler to find the length, width, and height of each of the rectangular objects. Have them estimate each length to the nearest inch or half-inch.

- Have your child identify how much is held by each measuring cup. Challenge him or her to "prove" that two half-cups or four quarter-cups equal one cup.

Science Fun

This activity will give your child practice at describing different physical properties of matter, as well as reinforcing that observations are made using all the senses, not just the eyes.

What You Need

- blindfold
- several pieces of clothing with different textures
- pieces of food with distinct odors, each in a separate plastic bag

What to Do

1. Gather the materials.

2. Give your child each object. Have him or her tell you about the object without looking at it. If your child has trouble, ask questions such as, is it hard or soft? Is it smooth or rough?

3. After your child describes an object, have him or her guess what the object is. Keep track of correct guesses.

Activity Materials from Home

Dear Family Member:

To do the activities in this chapter, we will need some materials that you may have at home. Please note the items at the right. If possible, please send these things to school with your child.

Your help and support are appreciated!

____ **penny, nickel**
____ **marble**
____ **key**
____ **cotton balls**
____ **uncooked macaroni**
____ **twist ties**
____ **pepper**

Harcourt

La escuela y la casa

Harcourt Ciencias

Contenido del capítulo

Hoy comenzamos un nuevo capítulo de ciencias sobre las propiedades físicas de la materia. Examinaremos las propiedades físicas, esas cosas que se pueden observar con los sentidos. Veremos cómo agregarle o quitarle calor hace que se produzcan cambios en su estado y exploraremos diferentes maneras de medir la materia.

Destrezas del proceso científico

Medir es una manera de aprender sobre los materiales que nos rodean. Esta actividad le dará a su hijo(a) la práctica para hacer medidas sencillas de longitud y volumen.

Busque una regla, tazas de medir de diferentes volúmenes y varias cajas rectangulares como de CD o cintas y cajas de zapatos.

- Pida a su hijo(a) que use la regla para hallar la longitud, el ancho y la altura de cada uno de los objetos rectangulares. Pídale que estime cada longitud a la pulgada o media pulgada más cercana.

- Pida a su hijo(a) que identifique qué cantidad contiene cada taza de medir. Rételo(a) a "comprobar" que dos medias tazas o cuatro cuartos de taza es igual a una taza.

Diversión

Esta actividad le dará a su hijo(a) la práctica para describir diferentes propiedades físicas de la materia así como también reforzará que las observaciones son hechas usando todos los sentidos, no sólo los ojos.

Lo que necesitas

- venda para los ojos
- varios pedazos de tela con diferentes texturas
- pedazos de comida con distintos olores, cada uno en una bolsa de plástico separado

Lo que vas a hacer

1. Recopile con su hijo(a) los materiales.

2. Dé a su hijo(a) cada uno de los objetos. Pídale que le hable del objeto sin mirarlo. Si su hijo(a) tiene problemas, haga preguntas como: ¿Es duro o suave? ¿Es liso o áspero?

3. Después que su hijo(a) describa un objeto, pídale que adivine qué objeto es. Lleve la cuenta de las conjeturas correctas.

Materiales de casa para la actividad

Querido familiar:

Para hacer las actividades de este capítulo, necesitaremos algunos materiales que tal vez tenga en la casa. Observe los artículos de la lista de la derecha. Si es posible, por favor envíe estas cosas con su hijo(a) a la escuela.

¡Gracias por su ayuda y apoyo!

____ **moneda de 1 ¢, moneda de 5 ¢**
____ **canica**
____ **llave**
____ **bolitas de algodón**
____ **fideos crudos**
____ **alambritos**
____ **pimienta**

Harcourt

Chapter Content

In science we are beginning a chapter on how matter changes. We will examine physical changes, such as cutting, folding, and changing state. We will then compare these changes to chemical changes, in which matter is combined and different matter forms.

Science Process Skills

Your child is learning how to **observe** as scientists do. This activity will help your child observe physical changes that occur as you cook a meal.

Have your child help you plan and cook a simple meal such as spaghetti and salad. As you prepare each part of the meal, have your child identify any state changes that occur, such as water changing from a liquid to a gas as the spaghetti water boils. Also have your child discuss how the matter is changed physically as it is prepared. For example, salad ingredients are cut into small pieces, components for salad dressing may be mixed or shaken together, spaghetti changes from something hard to a soft, bendable material.

Science Fun

A mixture is a substance that contains two or more different types of matter. A tossed salad is a common mixture. In this activity, you can reinforce the properties of mixtures, and organize a portion of your home at the same time!

What to Do

1. Identify an area of your home that needs organizing. It may be a play area, a closet, a study area, or the kitchen junk drawer.

2. Work with your child to identify categories of matter to separate from the area. For example, in the kitchen junk drawer, you might wish to separate all the paper clips, rubber bands, and twist ties into separate containers.

3. Continue separating and organizing the parts of the mixture until the area is organized.

Activity Materials from Home

Dear Family Member:

To do the activities in this chapter, we will need some materials that you may have around your home. Please note the items listed at the right. If possible, please send these things to school with your child.

Your help and support are appreciated!

____ **marbles**
____ **rice**
____ **funnel**
____ **cookie sheet**
____ **large glass bowl**
____ **baking soda**
____ **vinegar**

Harcourt

La escuela y la casa

Contenido del capítulo

Harcourt Ciencias

Diversión

Hoy comenzamos un nuevo capítulo de ciencias sobre cómo cambia la materia. Examinaremos los cambios físicos como cortar, doblar y cambiar de estado. Luego compararemos estos cambios con los cambios químicos, en los cuales la materia se combina y se forman materias diferentes.

Una mezcla es una sustancia que contiene dos o más tipos de materia diferentes. Una ensalada es una mezcla común. En esta actividad, usted puede reforzar las propiedades de las mezclas y organizar una parte de su casa al mismo tiempo.

Destrezas del proceso científico

Su hijo(a) aprende a **observar** como lo hacen los científicos. Esta actividad ayudará a su hijo(a) a observar los cambios físicos que ocurren mientras usted prepara una comida.

Pida a su hijo(a) que lo ayude a preparar y cocinar una comida sencilla como espaguetis o ensalada. Mientras prepara cada parte de la comida, pida a su hijo(a) que identifique cualquier cambio de estado que ocurra, como el cambio del agua de líquido a gas, mientras el agua de los espaguetis está hirviendo. También pida a su hijo(a) que comente cómo cambia la sustancia físicamente mientras se prepara. Por ejemplo, los ingredientes de la ensalada se cortan en pedazos pequeños, los componentes de los aliños de la ensalada se pueden mezclar o revolver, los espaguetis cambian de algo duro a un material suave que se dobla.

Lo que vas a hacer

1. Identifique un área de su casa que necesite organizar. Puede ser un área de juego, un armario, un área de estudio o una gaveta de utensilios de cocina.

2. Trabaje con su hijo(a) para identificar categorías de la materia para separar del área. Por ejemplo, en la gaveta de utensilios de cocina, quizás desee separar todos los clips, elásticos y cierres en recipientes separados.

3. Continúe separando y organizando las partes de la mezcla hasta que el área esté organizada.

Materiales de casa para la actividad

Querido familiar:

Para hacer las actividades en este capítulo, necesitaremos algunos materiales que tal vez tenga en la casa. Observe los artículos de la lista de la derecha. Si es posible, por favor envíe estas cosas con su hijo(a) a la escuela.

¡Gracias por su ayuda y su apoyo!

____ **canicas**
____ **arroz**
____ **embudo**
____ **tazón grande de vidrio**
____ **bicarbonato**
____ **vinagre**

Harcourt

Chapter Content

Our science class is beginning a chapter on heat. We will learn the difference between heat and thermal energy, we will explore the ways that thermal energy moves, and we will investigate how temperature is measured.

Science Process Skills

A **hypothesis** is an educated guess about what causes an event. It is made based on what is known about the event. Scientists make hypotheses that they can test to learn about the world around them. You can give your child practice at making a hypothesis and then testing it as you eat breakfast!

Make pancakes. Have your child make a hypothesis about what will happen when he or she puts butter on the pancakes. Ask your child to explain why he or she made that hypothesis. Have your child test the hypothesis by putting butter on the cakes. Talk about how accurate the hypothesis was. Secretly give your child a cold pancake. Repeat the hypothesizing and testing, and reviewing. Compare the results. Discuss why it is important to test a hypothesis.

Science Fun

Lesson 2 of this chapter focuses on how thermal energy moves from place to place. In this activity you can observe the results of radiation, thermal energy that moves without touching anything.

What You Need

- glass jar with lid
- water
- 4 herbal tea bags

What to Do

1. Pour 1 liter (about 4 cups) of water into a glass jar.
2. Add 4 tea bags to the water and put the lid on the jar.
3. Place the jar in a sunny window.
4. After 3 or 4 hours, observe the jar. You have made sun tea! Add ice and serve in tall glasses.

Activity Materials from Home

Dear Family Member:

To do the activities in this chapter we will need some materials that you may have at home. Please note the items at the right. If possible, please send these things to school with your child.

Your help and support are appreciated!

_____ **metal button**
_____ **small pieces of wool**
_____ **wooden spoon**
_____ **plastic spoons**

Harcourt

La escuela y la casa

Contenido del capítulo

Hoy comenzamos un nuevo capítulo de ciencias sobre el calor. Aprenderemos la diferencia entre calor y energía térmica, exploraremos las formas en que se mueve la energía térmica e investigaremos cómo se mide la temperatura.

Destrezas del proceso científico

Una **hipótesis** es una adivinanza apollada por datos sobre lo que causa un evento. Ésta se hace basada en lo que se conoce sobre el evento. Los científicos formulan hipótesis que pueden comprobar para aprender sobre el mundo que los rodea. ¡Usted puede darle a su hijo(a) práctica para formular una hipótesis y luego probarla mientras toma el desayuno!

Haga panqueques. Pida a su hijo(a) que formule una hipótesis sobre qué pasará cuando coloque mantequilla sobre los panqueques. Pida a su hijo(a) que explique por qué formuló esa hipótesis. Pida a su hijo(a) que compruebe la hipótesis poniendo mantequilla sobre los panqueques. Hable sobre qué tan precisa fue la hipótesis. En secreto, dé a su hijo(a) un panqueque frío. Repita la hipótesis y la prueba. Compare los resultados. Comente por qué es importante comprobar una hipótesis.

Harcourt Ciencias

Diversión

La Lección 2 de este capítulo enfoca en cómo la energía térmica se mueve de un lugar a otro. En esta actividad puede observar los resultados de la radiación, la energía térmica que se mueve sin tocar nada.

Lo que necesitas

- frasco de vidrio con tapa
- agua
- 4 bolsas de té de hierba

Lo que vas a hacer

1. Coloca 1 litro (casi 4 tazas) de agua en un frasco de vidrio.
2. Agrega 4 bolsas de té al agua y ponle la tapa al frasco.
3. Coloca el frasco donde le dé el Sol.
4. Después de 3 ó 4 horas, observa el frasco. ¡Haz hecho té! Agrégale hielo y sírvelo en un vaso alto.

Materiales de casa para la actividad

Querido familiar:

Para hacer las actividades en este capítulo, necesitaremos algunos materiales que tal vez tenga en la casa. Observe los artículos de la lista de la derecha. Si es posible, por favor envíe estas cosas con su hijo(a) a la escuela.

¡Gracias por su ayuda y su apoyo!

_____ **botón de metal**
_____ **pedazos pequeños de lana**
_____ **cuchara de madera**
_____ **cucharas de plástico**

Harcourt

School-Home Connection

Chapter Content

In science, we are beginning a chapter on light. We will be discovering how light travels, what light can do, and how light and color are related. We will also explore reflection, refraction, and absorption of light.

Science Process Skills

Making careful **observations** is an important science skill. Choose among these ideas and have your child explain the property of light each game shows.

- **Shadow Puppets:** Direct a strong light at a blank wall. Use your hands to block the light and make animal pictures. (Solid objects block light.)

- **Flashlight Tag:** Give each player a flashlight. Have everyone stand in a dark, open area. Move around, and shine your flashlight on different objects. People who are "tagged" with light are out. (We only see objects when light reflects off them.)

- **Rainbow Hunt:** On a sunny day, look for rainbows in puddles, on windshields, or where light shines through glass or plastic prisms. (Light is made of many colors.)

Science Fun

Light bends as it moves from one medium, such as air, to another, such as water. This property of light is called refraction. Your child can use refraction to do this trick.

What You Need

- coin
- bowl with opaque sides
- water

What to Do

1. Place a coin in the bottom of the bowl. Have a partner step back from the bowl just until the coin can no longer be seen.

2. Slowly pour water into the bowl. What happens?

3. Repeat the trick, this time holding the coin in place with your finger. The coin and the fingertip will both appear as the water is poured into the bowl.

Activity Materials from Home

Dear Family Member:

To do the activities in this chapter, we will need some materials that you may have around your home. Please note the items listed at the right. If possible, please send these things to school with your child.

Your help and support are appreciated!

_____ index cards
_____ clay

Harcourt

La escuela y la casa

Contenido del capítulo

Hoy comenzamos un nuevo capítulo de ciencias sobre la luz. Descubriremos cómo viaja la luz, qué puede hacer la luz y cómo se relacionan la luz y el color. También exploraremos la reflexión, la refracción y la absorción de la luz.

Destrezas del proceso científico

Hacer **observaciones** detalladas es una destreza importante de las ciencias. Elija entre estas ideas y pida a su hijo(a) que explique la propiedad de la luz en cada uno de los juegos que se muestran.

- **Mascotas de sombras:** Dirija una luz fuerte hacia una pared en blanco. Use sus manos para bloquear la luz y hacer ilustraciones de animales. (Los objetos sólidos bloquean la luz.)

- **Marcar con una linterna:** Dé a cada jugador una linterna. Pida a cada uno que se pare en una área oscura y abierta. Muévase y alumbre diferentes objetos con su linterna. A la persona que se "marca" con la luz, está fuera. (Sólo vemos los objetos cuando la luz los refleja.)

- **Cacería de arco iris:** En un día soleado, busque arco iris en los charcos, en los parabrisas o donde la luz brilla a través de prismas de vidrio o plástico. (La luz es hecha de muchos colores.)

Diversión

La luz se inclina a medida que se mueve de un medio como el aire a otro como el agua. Esta propiedad de la luz se llama refracción. Su hijo(a) puede usar la refracción para hacer este truco.

Lo que necesitas

- una moneda
- tazón con lados opacos
- agua

Lo que vas a hacer

1. Coloca una moneda en el fondo del tazón. Pide a un compañero que se aleje del tazón hasta que ya no pueda ver la moneda.

2. Vierte despacio agua en el tazón. ¿Qué sucede?

3. Repite el truco, esta vez sostén la moneda con tu dedo. La moneda y la punta del dedo aparecerán mientras se vierte el agua en el tazón.

Materiales de casa para la actividad

Querido familiar:

Para hacer las actividades en este capítulo, necesitaremos algunos materiales que tal vez tenga en la casa. Observe los artículos de la lista de la derecha. Si es posible, por favor envíe estas cosas con su hijo(a) a la escuela.

¡Gracias por su ayuda y su apoyo!

_____ tarjetas
_____ plastilina

Harcourt

School-Home Connection

Harcourt Science

Chapter Content

Our science class is beginning a chapter on forces and motion. We will be studying what causes motion and how forces can change the motion of an object. We will also be investigating the scientific definition of *work*. The chapter ends by exploring kinds of simple machines and how they help people do work.

Science Process Skills

Learning how to **interpret data** is a skill in science. When you interpret data, you look at the data and try to find trends.

Set up a simple ramp using a long board. Have your child experiment by rolling a car down the ramp. Have him or her change the height of the ramp (raise or lower), the weight of the cars (tape coins or washers on the cars to increase the weight), or the texture of the ramp (cover with sandpaper or carpet, rub with wax paper). Collect data on the time it takes for the car to roll down the ramp, or how far past the end of the ramp the car travels. After several trials, work with your child to interpret the data. In general, you should find that heavier cars, smoother surfaces, and higher ramps cause faster speeds.

Science Fun

An inclined plane is a flat surface set at an angle to another surface. An inclined plane, such as a ramp, is an example of a simple machine. This activity will help your child explore the uses of this simple machine.

What to Do

Go on a ramp scavenger hunt to see how inclined planes help people do work. Here are some places you might visit:

- Go to the post office to watch how mail is loaded and unloaded.

- Take note of how many intersections have converted the sidewalk-crossing corner into a ramp for wheelchairs.

- Visit libraries, museums, and markets and identify the ramps that allow for wheelchair access.

- Note any ramps being used by people delivering goods from trucks.

When you are finished, analyze the data you gathered. Where are ramps used most often? What is their purpose? Where should ramps be installed?

Activity Materials from Home

Dear Family Member:

To do the activities in this chapter, we will need some materials that you may have at home. Please note the items at the right. If possible, please send these things to school with your child.

Your help and support are appreciated!

_____ **string**
_____ **wooden board (about 1 m long)**

Harcourt

La escuela y la casa

Harcourt Ciencias

Contenido del capítulo

Hoy comenzamos un nuevo capítulo de ciencias sobre las fuerzas y el movimiento. Estudiaremos lo que causa el movimiento y cómo las fuerzas pueden cambiar el movimiento de un objeto. También investigaremos la definición científica de *trabajo*. El capítulo finaliza explorando los tipos de máquinas sencillas y cómo éstas ayudan a trabajar a las personas.

Destrezas del proceso científico

Aprender cómo **interpretar datos** es una destreza de ciencias. Cuando interpretas datos, miras los datos y tratas de hallar tendencias.

Arme una rampa sencilla usando una tabla larga. Pida a su hijo(a) que experimente rodando un carro por la rampa. Pídale que cambie la altura de la rampa (subir o bajar), el peso de los carros (pegar monedas o tuercas para aumentar el peso) o la textura de la rampa (cubrir con papel de lija o alfombra, frotar con papel encerado). Recopile datos del tiempo que tarda el carro en rodar por la rampa o qué distancia recorre el carro al pasar el final de la rampa. Después de varios intentos, trabaje con su hijo(a) para interpretar los datos. En general, deberían determinar que los carros más pesados, las superficies más lisas y las rampas más altas producen velocidades más rápidas.

Diversión

Un plano inclinado es una superficie plana puesta en un ángulo con otra superficie. Un plano inclinado como una rampa, es un ejemplo de una máquina sencilla. Esta actividad ayudará a su hijo(a) a explorar los usos de esta máquina sencilla.

Lo que vas a hacer

Con su hijo(a), salgan en busca de rampas para determinar cómo los planos inclinados ayudan a trabajar a las personas. Aquí hay algunos lugares que podrían visitar:

- Vayan a la oficina de correos para observar cómo se carga y se descarga el correo.
- Tomen nota de cuántas intersecciones han convertido a la esquina de cruce en una rampa para sillas de rueda.
- Visiten bibliotecas, museos y supermercados e identifiquen las rampas que permiten el acceso a sillas de ruedas.
- Fíjense en cualquier rampa que usan las personas que entregan bienes con camiones.

Cuando terminen, analicen los datos que recopilaron. ¿Dónde se usan las rampas más a menudo? ¿Cuál es su propósito? ¿Dónde se deben instalar las rampas?

Materiales de casa para la actividad

Querido familiar:

Para hacer las actividades en este capítulo, necesitaremos algunos materiales que tal vez tenga en la casa. Observe los artículos de la lista de la derecha. Si es posible, por favor envíe estas cosas con su hijo(a) a la escuela.

¡Gracias por su ayuda y su apoyo!

_____ hilo
_____ tabla de madera
(casi de 1 m de largo)

Harcourt

Picture Cards

Card #1
Canada goose

Card #2
albatross chick

Card #3
hermit crab

Card #4
armadillo

Harcourt

Picture Cards

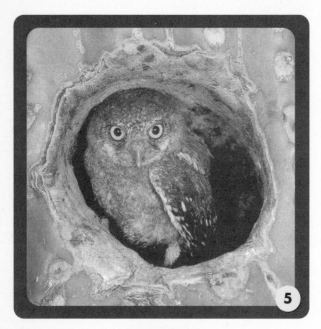

Card #5
elf owl

Card #6
gray foxes

Card #7
prairie dog

Card #8
snakes

Harcourt

Picture Cards

Card #9
bees

Card #10
termites and a termite mound

Card #11
bats

Card #12
beaver

Harcourt

Picture Cards

Card #13
osprey

Card #14
young polar bear

Card #15
newt

Card #16
oysters on mangrove roots

Picture Cards

Card #17
wasps

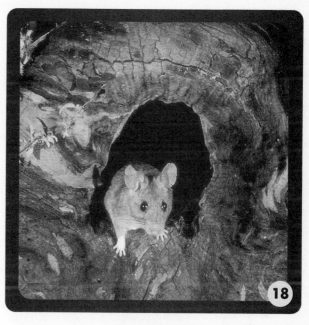

Card #18
wood rat

Card #19
mountain lion

Card #20
eel in coral

Picture Cards

Card #21
rock quarry with blocks of marble

Card #22
oil derrick

Card #23
tilled field

Card #24
forest

Picture Cards

Card #25
iron ore

Card #26
marble statues

Card #27
car being filled at gasoline pump

Card #28
corn

Picture Cards

Card #29
wooden house frames

Card #30
steel bridge

Card #31
gravel road

Card #32
garden path

Picture Cards

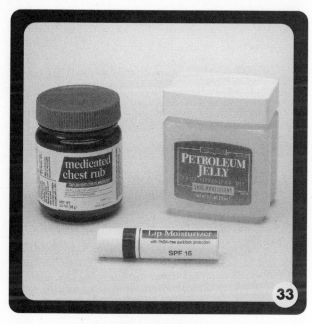

Card #33
personal care products

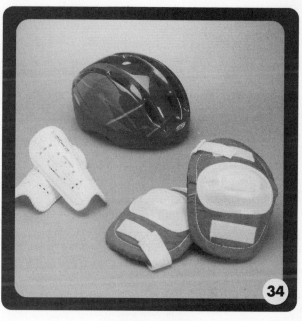

Card #34
plastic sports equipment

Card #35
blue jeans, cotton balls, towels

Card #36
flowers

Picture Cards

Card #37
furniture

Card #38
notebook

Card #39
iron fence

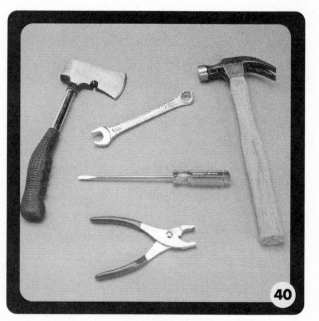

Card #40
tools

Harcourt

Writing in Science

Model: Research Report Outline

To write a **research report,** a writer gathers facts from several sources, takes notes, and makes an **outline.** The notes and outline are used to write the report. The writer lists the sources at the end of the report.

Outline

An outline follows a certain form. Roman numerals show the main ideas. Letters show the subtopics.

Scientists Predict Volcanic Eruptions

I. Information studied
   A. Volcano's history
   B. Rising ground
   C. Gases in the air
II. Kinds of warnings
   A. Before eruption
   B. Volcano drills

Writing in Science

Model: Research Report

A **research report** gives facts about a topic. This short report follows the outline on page TR 43. Reports can be several pages long.

title	Scientists Predict Volcanic Eruptions
main topic **facts** **about** **subtopics**	Scientists are getting better at telling when a volcano will erupt. One way they can tell is to study how often it has erupted before. Another way they can tell is to use a special instrument called a tiltmeter. They use this instrument to measure whether the ground is rising. Scientists also use an instrument called a gas detector. It measures the amount of gas in the air.
main topic **facts** **about** **subtopics**	When scientists think an eruption is coming, they warn people and tell them to leave. In parts of Japan and Ecuador, towns conduct volcano drills. These are like fire drills. Scientists have saved many lives with their research.

Vocabulary Cards

leaf	chlorophyll
root	photosynthesis
stem	inherit
seed	trait
seedling	mammal
germinate	bird

Harcourt

[klôr′ə·fil′] The substance that gives plants their green color; it helps a plant use energy from the sun to make food (A20)	[lēf] A plant part that grows out of the stem; it takes in the air and light that a plant needs (A7)
[fōt′ō·sin′thə·sis] The food-making process of plants (A20)	[rōōt] The part of a plant that holds the plant in the ground and takes in water and minerals from the soil (A7)
[in·her′it] To receive traits from parents (A38)	[stem] A plant part that connects the roots with the leaves of a plant; it carries water from the roots to other parts of the plant (A7)
[trāt] A body feature that an animal inherits; it can also be some things that an animal does (A38)	[sēd] The first stage in the growth of many plants (A12)
[mam′əl] An animal that has fur or hair and is fed milk from its mother's body (A42)	[sēd′ling] A young plant (A13)
[bûrd] An animal that has feathers, two legs, and wings (A45)	[jûr′mə·nāt′] When a new plant breaks out of the seed (A13)

amphibian	ecosystem
reptile	community
scales	population
fish	habitat
gills	forest
environment	deciduous forest

[ek′ō·sis′təm] **The living and nonliving things in an environment (B7)**	[am·fĭb′ē·ən] **An animal that begins life in the water and moves onto land as an adult (A50)**
[kə·myōō′nə·tē] **All the populations of organisms that live in an ecosystem (B7)**	[rep′tĭl] **A land animal that has dry skin covered by scales (A55)**
[pop′yōō·lā′shən] **A group of the same kind of living things that all live in one place at the same time (B7)**	[skālz] **The small, thin, flat plates that help protect the bodies of fish and reptiles (A52)**
[hab′ə·tat′] **The place where a population lives in an ecosystem (B7)**	[fish] **An animal that lives its whole life in water and breathes with gills (A52)**
[fôr′ist] **An area in which the main plants are trees (B12)**	[gilz] **A body part found in fish and young amphibians that takes in oxygen from the water (A51)**
[dē·sij′ōō·əs fôr′ist] **A forest in which most of the trees lose and regrow their leaves each year (B13)**	[in·vī′rən·mənt] **The things, both living and non-living, that surround a living thing (B6)**

—Harcourt

coastal forest	producer
coniferous forest	decomposer
tropical rain forest	consumer
desert	interact
fresh water	energy pyramid
salt water	food chain

[prə·dōōs′ər] **A living thing that makes its own food (B43)**	[kōs′təl fôr′ist] **A thick forest with tall trees that gets a lot of rain and does not get very warm or cold (B15)**
[dē′kəm·pōz′er] **A living thing that breaks down dead organisms for food (B44)**	[kō·nif′ər·əs fôr′ist] **A forest in which most of the trees are conifers (cone-bearing) and stay green all year (B16)**
[kən·sōōm′ər] **A living thing that eats other living things as food (B43)**	[trop′i·kəl rān′fôr′ist] **A hot, wet forest where the trees grow very tall and their leaves stay green all year (B14)**
[in′tər·akt′] **When plants and animals affect one another or the environment to meet their needs (B42)**	[dez′ərt] **An ecosystem where there is very little rain (B20)**
[en′ər·jē pir′ə·mid] **A diagram that shows that the amount of useable energy in an ecosystem is less for each higher animal in the food chain (B50)**	[fresh′ wôt′ər] **Water that has very little salt in it (B26)**
[fōōd′ chān′] **The path of food from one living thing to another (B48)**	[sôlt′ wô′tər] **Water that has a lot of salt in it (B26)**

predator	mineral
prey	rock
food web	rock cycle
core	metamorphic rock
crust	sedimentary rock
mantle	igneous rock

[min′ər·əl] **An object that is solid, is formed in nature, and has never been alive (C6)**	[pred′ə·tər] **An animal that hunts another animal for food (B54)**
[rok] **A solid made of minerals (C8)**	[prā] **An animal that is hunted by a predator (B54)**
[rok′ sī′kəl] **The process in which one type of rock changes into another type of rock (C14)**	[fo͞od′ web′] **A model that shows how food chains overlap (B54)**
[met′ə·môr′fik rok′] **A rock that has been changed by heat and pressure (C12)**	[kôr] **The center of the Earth (C8)**
[sed′ə·men′tər·ē rok′] **A rock formed from material that has settled into layers and been squeezed until it hardens into rock (C12)**	[krust] **The solid outside layer of the Earth (C8)**
[ig′nē·əs rok′] **A rock that was once melted rock but has cooled and hardened (C12)**	[man′təl] **The middle layer of the Earth (C8)**

fossil	valley
barrier island	mountain
plain	weathering
canyon	erosion
plateau	glacier
landform	earthquake

[val'ē] A landform; a lowland area between higher lands, such as mountains (C35)	[fos'əl] Something that has lasted from a living thing that died long ago (C20)
[moun'tən] A landform; a place on Earth's surface that is much higher than the land around it (C35)	[bar'ē·ər ī'lənd] A landform; a thin island along a coast (C35)
[we̱h'ər·ing] The process by which rock is worn down and broken apart (C40)	[plān] A landform; a flat area on Earth's surface (C35)
[i·rō'zhən] The movement of weathered rock and soil (C42)	[kan'yən] A landform; a deep valley with very steep sides (C35)
[glā'shər] A huge sheet of ice (C44)	[pla·tō'] A landform; a flat area higher than the land around it (C35)
[ûrth'kwāk'] The shaking of Earth's surface caused by movement of the crust and mantle (C48)	[land'fôrm'] A natural shape or feature of Earth's surface (C34)

Harcourt

volcano	loam
flood	resource
topsoil	conservation
soil	contour plowing
humus	strip cropping
clay	nonrenewable resource

[lōm] **A type of topsoil that is rich in minerals and has lots of humus (C70)**	[vol·kā′nō] **An opening in Earth's surface from which lava flows (C49)**
[rē′sôrs] **A material that is found in nature and that is used by living things (C88)**	[flud] **A large amount of water that covers normally dry land (C50)**
[kon′ser·vā′shən] **The saving of resources by using them carefully (C76)**	[top′soil′] **The top layer of soil made up of the smallest grains and the most humus (C63)**
[kon′tōōr plou′ing] **A type of plowing for growing crops; creates rows of crops around the sides of a hill instead of up and down (C76)**	[soil] **The loose material in which plants can grow in the upper layer of Earth (C62)**
[strip′ krop′ing] **A type of planting that uses strips of thick grass or clover between strips of crops (C76)**	[hyōō′məs] **The part of the soil made up of decayed parts of once-living things (C62)**
[non′ri·nōō′ə·bəl rē′sôrs] **A resource; such as coal or oil, that will be used up someday (C96)**	[klā] **A type of soil made up of very small grains; it holds water well (C69)**

Harcourt

renewable resource	condensation
inexhaustible resource	precipitation
recycle	water cycle
estuary	weather
groundwater	atmosphere
evaporation	anemometer

Harcourt

[kon´dən·sā´shən] **The changing of a gas into a liquid (D17)**	[ri·noo´ə·bəl rē´sôrs] **A resource that can be replaced in a human lifetime (C94)**
[prē·sip´ə·tā´shən] **The water that falls to Earth as rain, snow, sleet, or hail (D18)**	[in´eg·zôs´tə·bəl rē´sôrs] **A resource such as air or water that can be used over and over and can't be used up (C94)**
[wôt´ər sī´kəl] **The movement of water from Earth's surface into the air and back to the surface again (D19)**	[rē·sī´kəl] **To reuse a resource to make something new (C100)**
[weth´ər] **The happenings in the atmosphere at a certain time (D32)**	[es´choo·er´·ē] **A place where fresh water from a river mixes with salt water from the ocean (D12)**
[at´məs·fir´] **The air that surrounds Earth (D30)**	[ground´ wôt´ər] **A form of fresh water that is found under Earth's surface (D8)**
[an´ə·mom´ə·tər] **An instrument that measures wind speed (D40)**	[ē·vap´ə·rā´shən] **The process by which a liquid changes into a gas (D17, E18)**

Harcourt

front	planet
wind	orbit
temperature	solar system
weather map	axis
comet	rotation
asteroid	revolution

[plan′it] A large body of rock or gas that orbits the sun (D58)	**[frunt]** A place where two air masses of different temperatures meet (D37)
[ôr′bit] The path an object takes as it moves around another object in space (D58)	**[wind]** The movement of air (D40)
[sō′lər sis′təm] The sun, and the objects that orbit around it (D58)	**[tem′pər·ə·chər]** The measure of how hot or cold something is (D36)
[ak′sis] An imaginary line that goes through the North Pole and the South Pole of Earth (D68)	**[weth′ər map′]** A map that shows weather data for a large area (D46)
[rō·tā′shən] The spinning of an object on its axis (D68)	**[kom′it]** A large ball of ice and dust that orbits the sun (D64)
[rev′ə·lōō′shən] The movement of one object around another object (D68)	**[as′tər·oid]** A chunk of rock that orbits the sun (D64)

Harcourt

solar eclipse	solid
phases	liquid
lunar eclipse	gas
star	matter
constellation	physical property
telescope	atom

Harcourt

[sol′id] A form of matter that takes up a specific amount of space and has a definite shape (E11)	[sō′lər i·klips′] The hiding of the sun that occurs when the moon passes between the sun and Earth (D80)
[lik′wid] A form of matter that has volume that stays the same, but can change its shape (E12)	[fāz·əz] The different shapes the moon seems to have in the sky when observed from Earth (D76)
[gas] A form of matter that does not have a definite shape or a definite volume (E12)	[lōō′nər i·klips′] The hiding of the moon when it passes through the Earth's shadow (D78)
[mat′ər] Anything that takes up space (E6)	[stär] A hot ball of glowing gases, like our sun (D84)
[fiz′i·kəl prop′ər·tē] Anything you can observe about an object by using your senses (E6)	[kon′stə·lā′shən] A group of stars that form a pattern (D84)
[at′əm] The basic building block of matter (E16)	[tel′ə·skōp′] An instrument used to see faraway objects (D88)

Harcourt

evaporation	chemical change
volume	energy
mass	heat
solution	thermal energy
mixture	insulator
physical change	conductor

[kem′i·kəl chānj′]
A change that forms different kinds of matter (E46)

[ē·vap′ə·rā′shən]
The process by which a liquid changes into a gas (D17, E18)

[en′ər·jē]
The ability to cause change (F6)

[vol′yo͞om]
The amount of space that matter takes up (E22)

[hēt]
The movement of thermal energy from one place to another (F8)

[mas]
The amount of matter in an object (E24)

[thûr′məl en′ər·jē]
The energy that moves the particles in matter (F7)

[sə·lo͞o′shən]
A mixture in which the particles of two different kinds of matter mix together evenly (E42)

[in′sə·lāt′ər]
A material in which thermal energy does not move easily (F15)

[miks′chər]
A substance that contains two or more different types of matter (E41)

[kən·duk′tər]
A material in which thermal energy moves easily (F15)

[fiz′i·kəl chānj]
A change to matter in which no new kinds of matter are formed (E40)

thermometer	motion
absorption	gravity
reflection	weight
refraction	speed
prism	work
force	inclined plane

[mō′shən] **A change in position (F59)**	[thûr·mom′ə·tər] **A tool used to measure temperature (F20)**
[grav′i·tē] **The force that pulls objects toward each other (F62)**	[ab·sôrp′shən] **The stopping of light (F40)**
[wāt] **The measure of the pull of gravity on an object (F62)**	[ri·flek′shən] **The bouncing of light off an object (F36)**
[spēd] **The measure of how fast something moves over a certain distance (F61)**	[ri·frak′shən] **The bending of light when it moves from one kind of matter to another (F38)**
[wûrk] **The measure of force that it takes to move an object a certain distance (F66)**	[priz′əm] **A solid,transparent object that bends light into colors (F44)**
[in·klīnd′ plān′] **A simple machine made of a flat surface set at an angle to another surface (F71)**	[fôrs] **A push or a pull (F58)**

lever	
simple machine	

	[lev′ər] **A bar that moves on or around a fixed point (F70)**
	[sim′pəl mə·shēn′] **A tool that helps people do work (F70)**

Harcourt

Name _____ Date _____

What Stems Do

How does water move through a stem?

Materials
- 3 1-L plastic bottles
- water
- food coloring
- 3 freshly cut white carnations
- scissors

Procedure

❶ Fill the plastic bottles with water. Add a few drops of food coloring. Put a different color in each bottle.

❷ **CAUTION** **Be careful when using scissors.** Trim the end off the stem of each flower. Place one flower in each bottle.

❸ Keep the flowers in the bottles overnight. Then observe the flowers.

Draw Conclusions

Explain your observations. Make a bouquet of flowers with the colors you like best.

Growing Plants

Can plant parts be used to grow a new plant?

Materials
- 1 plant with many stems and leaves
- scissors
- 1-L plastic bottle
- water
- ruler

Procedure

❶ **CAUTION** **Be careful when using scissors.** Cut off a 15-cm piece of the plant.

❷ Fill the plastic bottle with water. Place the cut part of the plant in the bottle.

❸ Place the plant in bright sunlight.

Draw Conclusions

Observe the plant for ten days. Record any changes you observe.

A27

Harcourt

Name _____ Date _____

Shell Study

Why is a spiral shell larger at one end?

Materials

- safety goggles
- gloves
- spiral shell from an animal such as a whelk, conch, or sea snail
- coarse sandpaper
- hand lens

Procedure

❶ **CAUTION** Put on the safety goggles and gloves. Observe the outside of the shell. Rub the tip of the shell with sandpaper until you have a hole about 5 millimeters (about $\frac{1}{4}$ in.) wide.

❷ Use the hand lens to observe the inside of the shell. What do you see?

Draw Conclusions

Animals that live in spiral shells usually keep their shells for their whole lives. When they begin their lives, they are very small. Their shells are very small too.

Think about the shell you observed. Why do you think the spiral is small at one end and gets bigger at the other end?

Feather Study

What are the parts of feathers?

Materials

- 1 or 2 types of feathers from a bird
- hand lens

Procedure

❶ Study the feathers. Use the hand lens to look at their parts. Record what you observe.

❷ Touch the feathers as you look at them. Record what you feel.

Draw Conclusions

Discuss what you know about birds. Think of ways the feathers help birds fly.

A61

Harcourt

Earthworm Habitat

What is the habitat of an earthworm?

Materials

- clear plastic container
- garden soil (not potting soil)
- 2 to 3 earthworms
- small rocks, sticks, and leaves
- wax paper
- water

Procedure

1 Loosely spread the soil on the wax paper. Add the rocks, sticks, and leaves. Add a small amount of water so the soil is moist but not wet. Mix these materials together.

2 Add the soil mixture to the plastic container. Carefully add the earthworms to the loose soil. Place your earthworm habitat in a warm, dark place. Keep the soil moist.

Draw Conclusions

After observing your earthworm habitat for a week, make a list of the things you think the habitat you provided gave your earthworms that they needed to live.

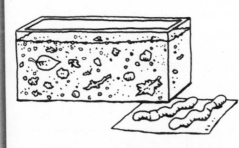

Salt Water and Fresh Water

How are salt water and fresh water different?

Materials

- small jar
- water
- egg in the shell
- small spoon
- salt

Procedure

1 Half fill the jar with water. Put the egg in the jar. Record what happens to the egg.

2 Remove the egg, and stir a spoonful of salt into the water. Put the egg back into the water, and record what happens to the egg.

3 Continue adding salt to the water until you observe a change.

Draw Conclusions

How do you think salt in the water affects the animals living in the ocean?

B35

Harcourt

Name _____ Date _____

Food Chains

How do animals get their food?

Materials
- name tags
- colored game markers
- small plastic bags

Procedure
Play this game with ten or more people.

❶ Have each player wear a tag that names him or her as a grasshopper, a snake, or a hawk. Scatter the game markers over a large area. The game markers are food.

❷ Each round of the game is 30 seconds. In the first round, only grasshoppers play. They collect as many markers as they can and put them in their bags.

❸ In the next round, only snakes play.

❹ In the final round, only hawks play.

Draw Conclusions
Which animals had the most food after three rounds? Talk about your answer.

Energy Flow

How does energy flow through a food chain?

Materials
- index cards
- crayons
- pushpins
- yarn

Procedure
❶ Divide the class into five groups: producers, plant eaters, plant and animal eaters, animal eaters, and decomposers.

❷ Have each person in your group draw on an index card and label a kind of plant or animal that is from your group.

❸ Form teams made up of one member from each group. Each team should make a food chain with the pictures. Use yarn to connect the parts on a bulletin board.

Draw Conclusions
How does energy flow through the food chain?

B61

Harcourt

Name _____ Date _____

Growing Crystals

How do salt crystals grow?

Materials

- salt
- hand lens
- hot tap water
- small jar
- plastic spoon
- small nail
- cotton string
- pencil

Procedure

❶ Observe the salt with the hand lens. Record what you see.

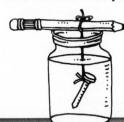

❷ **CAUTION** Be careful with hot water. Fill your jar with hot water. Add salt one spoonful at a time. Stir. Keep adding salt until no more will dissolve.

❸ Set up the jar as shown. The nail should not touch the jar.

❹ Leave the jar for five days. Then describe what you see on the nail and string.

Draw Conclusions

Observe this material with the hand lens. Compare it with the salt crystals you examined in Step 1.

Minerals in Sand

What minerals are found in sand?

Materials

- sand
- sheet of paper
- hand lens
- toothpick
- mineral descriptions

Procedure

❶ Spread the sand on a sheet of paper.

❷ Observe the colors and shapes of the sand grains with the hand lens. Each type of mineral grain has a different color and shape.

❸ Use the toothpick to move the grains of each mineral into a separate pile.

Draw Conclusions

Identify the minerals. Use the descriptions your teacher gives you. Which mineral is the most common?

C27

Shake the Earth

What are some effects of earthquakes?

Materials

- baking pan filled with gelatin
- plastic wrap
- large croutons

Procedure

❶ Cover the top of the gelatin with plastic wrap.

❷ Use croutons to make buildings on top of the gelatin.

❸ Move the pan up and down. Then move the pan from side to side. Then tap one end of the pan as you move it. Observe the movement of the gelatin.

Draw Conclusions

Did the movement damage your buildings? **Record** your observations. How is this model like an earthquake?

Weathering

Can chemicals in water wear away rock?

Materials

- 6 small glass jars without labels
- wax pencil
- 3 types of rock chips (limestone, sandstone, quartzite)
- water
- white vinegar

Procedure

❶ Label two jars *limestone*. Write *sandstone* on two jars. Write *quartzite* on the last two jars.

❷ Put a few rock chips in each jar. Make sure the chips match the jar's label.

❸ Fill one jar of each pair with water. Fill the other jar with vinegar.

❹ Observe what happens. Wait 30 minutes, and observe again. Let the jars sit overnight. Then, observe them again.

Draw Conclusions

How did the vinegar and the water affect the rocks?

C55

Name _____ Date _____

Soil and Plants

How does soil help plants grow?

Materials

- 4 plants of the same kind
- potting soil
- sand
- water
- measuring cup
- ruler

Procedure

❶ Take the plants from their store pots. Dump out the soil. Rinse the roots.

❷ Put each plant back into its empty pot. Put potting soil around two plants. Put sand around the other two plants. Water each plant with the same amount of water.

❸ Put the plants in the same sunny place. Use the measuring cup to give the plants the same amount of water each day.

❹ Observe the plants for 14 days. Measure their heights. Count the leaves.

Draw Conclusions

Which soil is best for growing the plants?

Food from Soil

Where do the foods you eat come from?

Materials

- outline map of the United States
- an encyclopedia
- crayons or colored pencils

Procedure

❶ Get a map of the United States from your teacher.

❷ Make a list of some of the foods you like to eat. Find out where these foods are grown. Look up the information in an encyclopedia.

❸ Use the map to share your findings. Draw a picture of each food on your list. Glue each picture onto the map to show where the food is grown.

Draw Conclusions

Where do the foods you eat come from?

C81

How Much Waste?

How much waste does your class throw away each day?

Materials

- paper
- pencil

What We Threw Away Today	
Newspaper and Magazines	
Cardboard and Other Paper	
Glass Containers	
Plastic Containers	
Plastic Wrapping and Bags	
Other	

Procedure

❶ Copy one chart for the class. Put the chart and a pencil next to the trash can.

❷ All students in your class should record what they throw away. If a paper is thrown away, then a *1* is written in the Paper row. If 3 plastic bottles are thrown away, then *3 bottles* is written in the Plastic Containers row.

Draw Conclusions

After gathering data for one day, total all the things that were thrown away. How could your class recycle more?

Reuse It!

How can some classroom materials be reused?

Materials

- large cardboard or plastic boxes
- black marking pen
- tape

Procedure

❶ Use the chart from "How Much Waste?" As a class, decide which materials could be reused instead of being thrown away. Work with your teacher to find a place in the room to store materials that can be reused.

❷ Find cardboard boxes or plastic bins for keeping the materials. Label each box with the material it will hold. Be sure that items that had food in them, such as plastic containers, are rinsed before being put in the boxes.

Draw Conclusions

After you have started your REUSE IT! center, check your trash again. How does the amount of trash compare with the amount of trash before the REUSE IT! center was started?

C109

Name _____ Date _____

Cloud in a Jar

How do raindrops form?

Materials

- metal pie pan
- freezer
- glass jar without lid
- hot water
- ice cubes

Procedure

❶ Put the pan in the freezer for an hour.

❷ Just before you take the pan out, have your teacher fill the jar half way with hot water.

❸ Remove the pan from the freezer, and fill it with ice cubes. Place the pan on top of the jar. Leave it there for a few minutes.

Draw Conclusions

Observe what happens inside the jar. How is this like part of the water cycle?

Making Raindrops

Why do raindrops fall?

Materials

- dropper
- water
- clear plastic coffee-can lid
- pencil

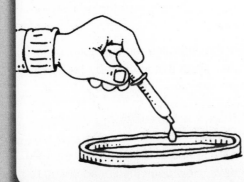

Procedure

❶ Fill the dropper with water.

❷ Turn the lid so the top of the lid rests flat on the table. Drop small drops of water onto the lid. Put as many drops as you can on the lid without having the drops touch.

❸ Quickly turn the lid over.

❹ Holding the lid upside down, move drops together with the pencil point. What happens?

Draw Conclusions

How is this similar to what happens in clouds?

D23

Name _____   Date _____

Measure Precipitation

How can you find out how much rain falls?

Materials
- masking tape
- ruler
- clear plastic 1-L bottle with top cut off

Procedure
❶ Tape the ruler to the outside of the bottle. The 1-in. mark should be at the bottom of the bottle.

❷ Put your rain gauge outside before it rains. Do not place it under a tree or under an object that might block the rain.

❸ Check the amount of water in the bottle after the rain stops.

Draw Conclusions
Look on the weather page of the newspaper. How much rain fell the day you used your gauge? Was your measurement correct? How close was your measurement?

Measure the Wind

How fast does the wind blow?

Materials
- 2 cardboard strips
- stapler
- cap of a ballpoint pen
- 4 small paper cups (3 white, 1 red)
- watch with second hand
- scissors
- wire

Procedure
❶ Make an X with the cardboard strips. Staple the strips together.

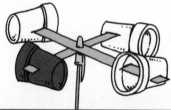

❷ Use the scissors to make a hole in the middle of the X. Push the pen cap into the hole as shown

❸ Cut a slit in the opposite sides of each cup. Attach the cups as shown.

❹ Push the piece of wire deep into the ground outside. Balance the pen cap on the wire.

❺ Count the times the red cup spins by in 1 minute. Divide this number by 10. The answer tells how many miles per hour the wind is blowing.

Draw Conclusions
Measure the speed of the wind over the next several days. How does the speed change?

D51

Name _____ Date _____

Earth Model

Why do we have seasons?

Materials
- Styrofoam ball
- flashlight
- two pencils

Procedure

1 Stick a pencil through the middle of the ball. This represents Earth's axis.

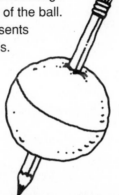

2 With the other pencil, draw a line around the middle of the ball. This is the equator. Put the Earth on a table. The axis should lean to the right.

3 Shine the flashlight on the left side of the Earth. The light represents the sun. Place the light about 13 cm away. Observe where the light rays hit the ball.

4 Shine the light on the right side of the Earth. Where do the light rays hit the ball? Compare how the light hits the ball each time.

Draw Conclusions
How does this explain seasons in the northern half of the Earth?

A Look at Rotation

How does day become night?

Materials
- a small self-stick note
- spinning Earth globe
- flashlight

Procedure

1 Write where you live on the self-stick note. Place the note on your state on the globe.

2 Shine the flashlight on the globe. Your teacher will then turn off the lights.

3 Slowly spin the globe counterclockwise.

Draw Conclusions
What happens to the place where you put your note? What does this represent?

D93

Name _____ Date _____

Properties of Metals

Which metals have magnetic properties?

Materials

- magnet
- penny
- piece of aluminum foil
- straight pin
- scissors
- dime
- paper clip

	Objects
Magnetic	
Non-Magnetic	Objects

Procedure

❶ Copy the chart onto a sheet of paper.

❷ Place the magnet close to the penny. Does the penny stick to the magnet? Write down the results on your chart.

❸ Repeat Step 2 for each of the other objects. Write down the results for each one on the chart.

Draw Conclusions

Study your completed chart. Are all metals attracted by a magnet? Which kinds are?

Mass of Liquids

Which of three liquids has the greatest mass?

Materials

- clear measuring cup
- water
- oil
- red vinegar

Procedure

❶ Will water float on oil? Or will oil float on water? Predict which liquid will float on the other.

❷ Pour some water into the measuring cup.

❸ Add some oil. Observe what happens to the oil. Write down your observations. Was your prediction correct?

❹ Will the vinegar float on the water? Make a prediction.

❺ Pour some red vinegar into the measuring cup. Let it stand still for five minutes. Write down your observations.

Draw Conclusions

The lightest liquid floats on the others. List the liquids from lightest to heaviest.

E33

Name _____ Date _____

Changes in Cooking

What happens to muffins as they bake?

Materials

- 1 box of muffin mix
- other needed ingredients
- mixing bowl
- spoon
- muffin pan

Procedure

❶ Read and follow the directions on the box of muffin mix.

❷ Halfway through the cooking time, open the oven or turn on the oven light and observe the muffins. Record your observations.

Draw Conclusions

What is happening to the muffins?

Making a Solution

Which works better, hot water or cold water?

Materials

- 2 small, heat-proof glass containers
- cold water
- spoon
- sugar
- clock with second hand
- warm water (from the tap)

Procedure

❶ Fill one container with cold water.

❷ Mix a spoonful of the sugar into the water. Stir until the sugar dissolves.

❸ Watch the clock to see how long it takes. Record the number of seconds it takes.

❹ Repeat Steps 1–3 using warm water.

Draw Conclusions

How were the results different? Why do you think they were different?

E53

Testing Insulators

Is wool or sand a better insulator?

Materials

- 1 small coffee can with plastic lid
- 2 wool socks
- scissors
- 1 long lab thermometer
- clock with a second hand
- hair dryer
- 3 cups of sand

Procedure

❶ Stuff the can with the socks. Put the lid on. Cut a small hole in the middle of the lid for the thermometer. Make sure the thermometer is surrounded by wool. After five minutes, read and record the temperature.

❷ Start the hair dryer. Warm the outside of the can. Watch the thermometer and the clock. See how long it takes the temperature to go up 10°C.

❸ Repeat using sand in the coffee can.

Draw Conclusions

Compare results. Which is the better insulator? How do you know?

Cooling Water

How long does it take for warm water to cool?

Materials

- 2 foam cups
- warm water
- measuring cup
- 2 thermometers
- clock with a second hand

Procedure

❶ Fill one cup with 1 cup of warm water. Fill the other cup with $\frac{1}{2}$ cup of warm water.

❷ In which cup will the water cool faster? Make a hypothesis to answer the question. Write down your hypothesis.

❸ Make a chart to record temperatures. Record the starting temperature in each cup. Then record the temperature of each cup every minute until one cup of water reaches room temperature.

Draw Conclusions

Was your hypothesis correct? Explain.

F27

Name _____   Date _____

Colors

What colors are reflected off different colors of paper?

Materials
- glue
- strips of colored construction paper
- prism

Procedure

❶ Glue strips of construction paper together in the order of the colors of the rainbow: red, orange, yellow, green, blue, and violet.

❷ Use a prism to separate the colors in sunlight. Aim the colors from the prism at the different colors of construction paper.

❸ Observe how the light from the prism is reflected by the different colors of construction paper.

Draw Conclusions

What colors from the prism are reflected from the green piece of construction paper? Explain.

Make a Periscope

How can you see around a corner?

Materials
- glue
- aluminum foil
- 2 index cards
- shoe box
- black construction paper

Procedure

❶ Glue aluminum foil, shiny side out, to the index cards to make mirrors. Make the foil as smooth as possible.

❷ Line the inside of the box with black paper. Cut out a hole in the bottom of the box, about 3 cm from one end. Cut a hole in the lid about 3 cm from one end.

❸ Fold the ends of the aluminum foil mirrors to make tabs. Then glue the aluminum-foil mirrors to the inside of the box as shown.

❹ Put the lid back on the box, and look through your periscope.

Draw Conclusions

How could you use a periscope to see around a corner?

F51

Name _____   Date _____

Movement from Air

How can you move a Ping Pong ball with your breath?

Materials
- Ping Pong ball
- 3 straws
- colorful tape

Procedure

❶ Work in groups of three. Each person needs a straw. Clear a space on the floor. With tape, mark a course on the floor. Make sure the course has some twists and turns in it.

❷ Put the Ping Pong ball at the beginning of the course. With your partners, blow on the ball to make it follow the path.

Draw Conclusions

From which angle did you blow to make the ball move farthest? Which made the ball move farther, blowing softly or blowing hard? Which made the ball move farther, blowing steadily or blowing in short puffs?

Measuring Weight

How can you make your own spring scale?

Materials
- paper cup
- a large, heavy rubber band
- 2 rulers   ■ tape
- string   ■ objects

Procedure

❶ With your pencil, punch two small holes on each side of the paper cup. Place the rubber band as shown. Thread a piece of string through each pair of holes in the cup and tie the cup to the rubber band.

❷ Hold the ruler straight, and have your partner use another ruler to measure the length of the rubber band from the top of the cup to the ruler.

❸ Compare the weights of different objects by putting them in the cup and measuring the length of the rubber band.

Draw Conclusions

How is the length of the rubber band related to the weight of the objects put in the cup?

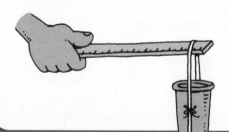

F77

PHYSICAL PROPERTIES CHARTS FOR WB 160

	It Looks				It Feels			
Object	Shiny	Dull	Color		Hard	Soft	Rough	Smooth
penny								
marble								
book								
index card								
key								
pepper								
nickel								
uncooked macaroni								
candy								
cotton								
twist tie								

	It Smells				It Sounds			
Object	Sweet	Sharp	No smell		Loud	Soft	Makes a ping	No sound
penny								
marble								
book								
index card								
key								
pepper								
nickel								
uncooked macaroni								
candy								
cotton								
twist tie								

Use with pages E4–E5.

Harcourt

Flowchart

```
┌─────────────────────────────────────────────┐
│                                               │
│                                               │
│                                               │
│                                               │
└─────────────────────────────────────────────┘
                      ↑
┌─────────────────────────────────────────────┐
│                                               │
│                                               │
│                                               │
│                                               │
└─────────────────────────────────────────────┘
                      ↑
┌─────────────────────────────────────────────┐
│                                               │
│                                               │
│                                               │
│                                               │
└─────────────────────────────────────────────┘
```

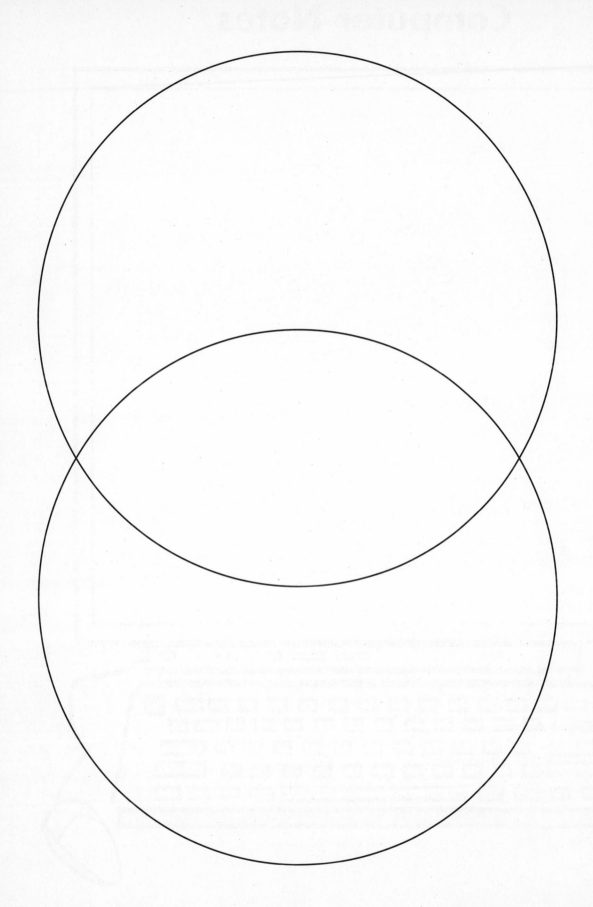

Venn Diagram

Computer Notes

K-W-L Chart

What I Know	What I Want to Know	What I Learned

Web

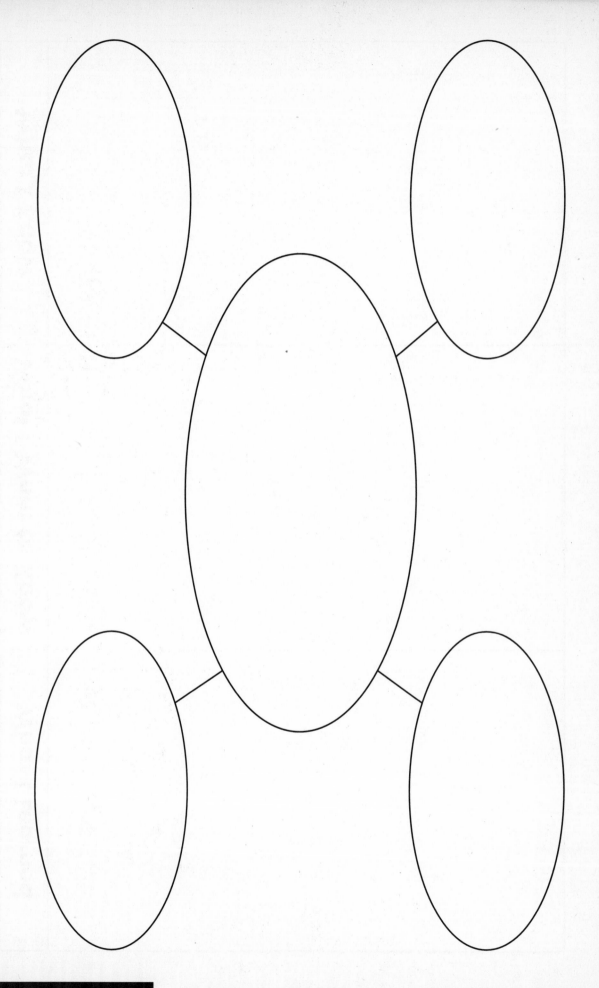

Chart

Knowledge Chart

Prior Knowledge About___	New Knowledge About___
1.	1.
2.	2.
3.	3.
4.	4.
5.	5.
6.	6.
7.	7.

Prediction Chart

What I Predict Will Happen	What Actually Happened

Project Plan

What We Want to Find Out

1.

How We Can Find Out

2.

What We Need to Do

3.   Materials

How We Can Share Information

4.

1-cm grid

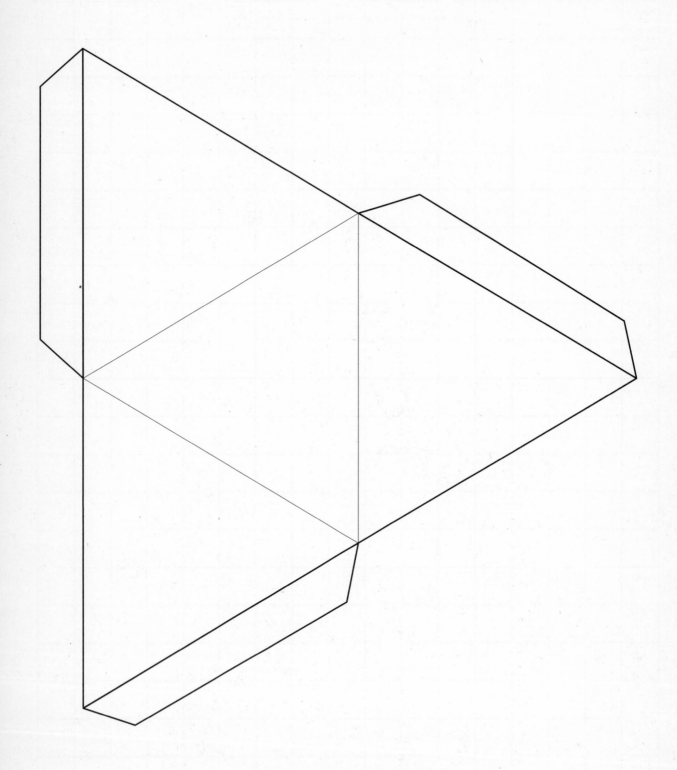

Use with page F45.

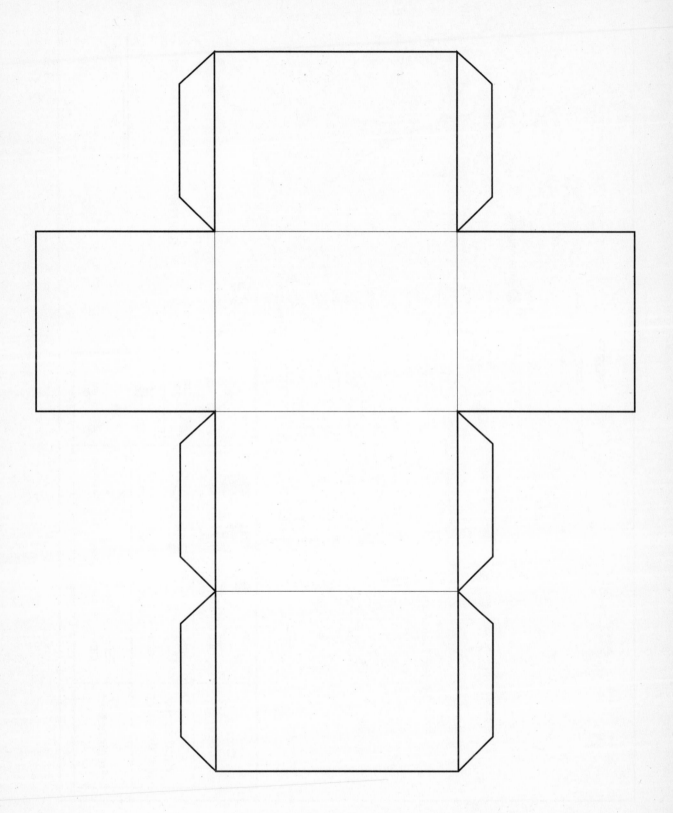

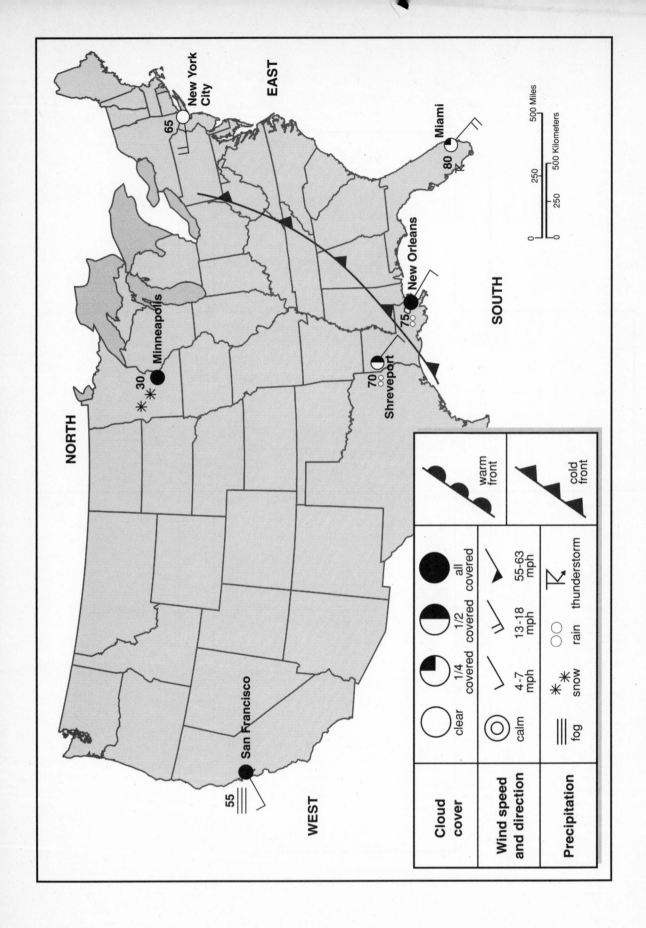

EAST

New York City
65

Miami
80

New Orleans
75

SOUTH

Minneapolis
30

Shreveport
70

NORTH

San Francisco
55

WEST

500 Miles
500 Kilometers
250
250

Cloud cover	clear	1/4 covered	1/2 covered	all covered
Wind speed and direction	calm	4-7 mph	13-18 mph	55-63 mph
Precipitation	fog	snow	rain	thunderstorm

warm front

cold front